Vegetables

BLOOMSBURY KITCHEN LIBRARY

Vegetables

Bloomsbury Books
London

This edition published 1994 by Bloomsbury Books,
an imprint of The Godfrey Cave Group,
42 Bloomsbury Street, London, WC1B 3QJ.

ISBN 1 85471 527 5

Printed and bound in Great Britain.

Contents

Artichoke Bottoms with Tomato and Rice

Serves 8

Working time: about 25 minutes

Total time: about 45 minutes

Calories 205

Protein 6g

Cholesterol 15mg

Total fat 9g

Saturated fat 4g

Sodium 190mg

4	artichoke bottoms	4
½	lemon	½
40 g	unsalted butter	1¼ oz
2 tbsp	virgin olive oil	2 tbsp
125 g	mushrooms, wiped and sliced	4 oz
¼ tsp	salt	¼ tsp
1	small onion, finely chopped	1
2 tsp	chopped fresh basil, or ¾ tsp dried basil	2 tsp
1	garlic clove, finely chopped	1
2	tomatoes, skinned, seeded and chopped	2
½ litre	unsalted chicken or vegetable stock	16 fl oz
175 g	rice	6 oz
	freshly ground black pepper	
60 g	Parmesan cheese, freshly grated	2 oz
10 g	Parsley, chopped	⅓ oz

Bring 1 litre (1¾ pints) of water to the boil. Squeeze the juice of the lemon into the water and add the lemon itself. Cook the artichoke bottoms in the boiling water for 10 minutes. Drain them and cut each into six wedges.

In a small saucepan, heat 15 g (½ oz) of the butter with the oil over medium heat. Add the mushrooms and salt, and sauté until the liquid from the mushrooms has evaporated. Stir in the onion and cook for 2 minutes, stirring frequently. Add the garlic, basil and tomatoes, and 12.5 cl (4 fl oz) of the stock. Bring to the boil, then reduce the heat and simmer for 10 minutes.

Remove the pan from the heat.

In a heavy, 4 litre (7 pint) saucepan, melt the remaining butter over medium-low heat. Add the rice and cook, stirring constantly, until the rice is opaque – 3 to 4 minutes. Stir in the vegetable mixture, ¼ litre (8 fl oz) of the stock and the pepper, and bring to the boil. Reduce the heat and simmer, covered, for 10 minutes.

Gently stir in the artichoke, the remaining stock and parmesan cheese, and continue to cook the dish, covered, until the rice is tender and the liquid is absorbed – 10 to 15 minutes.

Garnish with parsley; serve immediately.

Red Pepper and Tomato Sauce for Artichokes

Serves 4

Working time: about 30 minutes

Total time: about 1 hour and 30 minutes)

Calories 195

Protein 4g

Cholesterol 0mg

Total fat 14g

Saturated fat 1g

Sodium 170mg

4	artichokes, trimmed, cooked and chilled	4
1	large sweet red pepper	1
2½ tbsp	safflower oil	2½ tbsp
1½ tbsp	virgin olive oil	1½ tbsp
2	ripe tomatoes, skinned, seeded and coarsely chopped	2
1 tsp	tomato paste (optional)	1 tsp
1 tbsp	chopped shallot	1 tbsp
1	garlic clove, finely chopped	1
2 tbsp	chopped fresh basil, or 2 tsp dried basil	2 tbsp
1	spring onion, trimmed and chopped	1
2 tbsp	balsamic vinegar, or 1½ tbsp red wine vinegar mixed with ½ tsp honey	2 tbsp
¼ tsp	salt	¼ tsp
	freshly ground black pepper	

Peel the red pepper with a vegetable peeler, removing as much of the skin as possible. Seed and derib the pepper, and chop it coarsley.

In a heavy frying pan, heat the oils over medium heat. Add the red pepper, and lightly sauté for 2 minutes. Add the tomatoes, tomato paste, if you are using it, the shallot, garlic and basil, and cook, stirring frequently, until the red pepper is tender but still somewhat firm – about 5 minutes. Add the spring onion, the balsamic vinegar, salt and pepper, and simmer about 2 minutes, to bind the flavours and soften the red pepper.

Put the mixture into a food processor or blender, and purée. Chill for an hour and serve spooned on to the artichoke leaves.

Editor's Note: The sauce may also be used as a dip.

Artichoke and Red Pepper Sauté with Garlic

Serves 6

Working time: about 30 minutes

Total time: about 45 minutes

Calories 75
Protein 1g
Cholesterol 0mg
Total fat 7g
Saturated fat 1g
Sodium 100mg

4	artichoke bottoms	4
$\frac{1}{2}$	lemon	$\frac{1}{2}$
3 tbsp	virgin olive oil	3 tbsp
2	small garlic bulbs, cloves peeled, larger cloves halved lengthwise	2
$\frac{1}{4}$ tsp	salt	$\frac{1}{4}$ tsp
2	sweet red peppers	2

1$\frac{1}{2}$ tbsp	balsamic vinegar, or $\frac{3}{4}$ tbsp red wine vinegar mixed with $\frac{1}{4}$ tsp honey	1$\frac{1}{2}$ tbsp
1	shallot, finely chopped	1
$\frac{1}{2}$ tsp	fresh thyme, or $\frac{1}{8}$ tsp dried thyme	$\frac{1}{2}$ tsp
8	large fresh basil leaves, chopped, or $\frac{1}{2}$ tsp dried basil freshly ground black pepper	8

Fill a large non-reactive saucepan with water and bring it to a rolling boil. Squeeze the juice of the lemon into the water and add the lemon itself. Cook the artichoke bottoms in the boiling water until they can be pierced easily with the tip of a sharp knife – 12 to 14 minutes. Plunge the artichoke bottoms into cold water to arrest their cooking, then slice each into eight wedges.

Meanwhile, in a large, heavy frying pan, heat the oil over low heat. Add the garlic and cook it, stirring occasionally, until golden – about 30 minutes. Sprinkle with $\frac{1}{8}$ teaspoon of the salt. With a slotted spoon, transfer the garlic to a plate.

Peel the red peppers with a vegetable peeler, stripping away as much skin as possible. Seed, derib and slice the peppers into 5 mm ($\frac{1}{4}$ inch) strips.

Reheat the oil over medium heat. When it is hot, add the artichoke wedges and cook them gently for 3 minutes. Stir in the red pepper, vinegar, shallot, thyme and basil. Sprinkle with the remaining salt and the pepper, and cook for three minutes more. Return the garlic to the frying pan and combine it with the other ingredients. Serve immediately.

Stir-Fried Asparagus with Soy Sauce

Serves 4

Working time: about 25 minutes

Total time: about 30 minutes

Calories 85
Protein 4g
Cholesterol 0mg
Total fat 6g
Saturated fat 1g
Sodium 310mg

500 g	asparagus, trimmed and cut diagonally into 1 cm (½ inch) thick pieces	**1 lb**
2 tbsp	low-sodium soy sauce, or naturally fermented shoyu	**2 tbsp**
1½ tsp	finely chopped fresh ginger root	**1½ tsp**
1	garlic clove, finely chopped	**1**
1½ tbsp	dark sesame oil	**1½ tbsp**
1 tbsp	sesame seeds	**1 tbsp**

In a small bowl, combine the soy sauce, ginger and garlic, and set aside. In a wok or a large, heavy frying pan, heat the oil over medium-high heat. Add the soy mixture and the asparagus, and stir-fry for 3 minutes. Cover and steam the asparagus until just tender – about 2 minutes. Stir in the sesame seeds and serve immediately.

Baked Asparagus with Pine-Nuts and Gruyère

Serves 4

Working time: about 20 minutes

Total time: about 25 minutes

Calories 145
Protein 7g
Cholesterol 20mg
Total fat 13g
Saturated fat 4g
Sodium 50mg

500 g	medium asparagus, trimmed and peeled	**1 lb**
1 tsp	unsalted butter	**1 tsp**
60 g	grated Gruyère cheese	**2 oz**

3 tbsp	pine-nuts	**3 tbsp**
1 tbsp	virgin olive oil	**1 tbsp**
	freshly ground black pepper	

Preheat the oven to 180°C (350°F or Mark 4).

In a large, shallow fireproof casserole, melt the butter over medium heat. Line up the asparagus on the bottom, with the tips facing in one direction. Add 3 tablespoons of water and cover the casserole. Position it so that the thicker ends of the stalks are over the centre of the burner, and steam the asparagus for 2 minutes.

Remove the casserole from the heat, and sprinkle the cheese on the stems, but not the tips. Strew the pine-nuts on the cheese, then dribble the olive oil on top. Sprinkle the asparagus with pepper.

Place the casserole in the oven, and bake, uncovered, until the cheese has melted – about 5 minutes. Serve bubbling hot.

Sweet-and-Sour Celery

Serves 4

Working time: about 10 minutes

Total time: about 15 minutes

Calories 35
Protein 1g
Cholesterol 0mg
Total fat 0g
Saturated fat 0g
Sodium 265mg

1	head of celery, leaves removed, stalks cut on the diagonal into 2.5 cm (1 inch) slices	1	
1 tbsp	sugar	1 tbsp	
¼ tsp	salt	¼ tsp	

⅛ tsp	cayenne pepper	⅛ tsp	
6 cl	cider vinegar	2 fl oz	
1 tbsp	finely chopped sweet red pepper	1 tbsp	

Pour enough water into a large frying pan to fill it about 5 mm (¼ inch) deep. Add the celery, sugar, salt and cayenne pepper. Cover the pan, leaving the lid slightly off centre to vent steam, and bring the water to the boil. Cook until the celery is tender and the water has evaporated – about 5 minutes. Remove the pan from the heat and stir in the vinegar. Transfer the sweet-and-sour celery to a serving dish and scatter the chopped red pepper over the top. Serve immediately.

Marinated Cauliflower

Serves 6

Working time: about 20 minutes

Total time: about 1 hour

Calories 85

Protein 4g

Cholesterol 0mg

Total fat 5g

Saturated fat 1g

Sodium 105mg

1	cauliflower head, cut into florets	1
1	onion, sliced	1
3	lemons, juice only	3
5 cm	strip of lemon peel	2 inch
8	parsley sprigs	8
3	fresh thyme sprigs, or ¼ tsp dried thyme	3

1 tsp	coriander seeds	1 tsp
½ tsp	cumin seeds	½ tsp
¼ tsp	salt	¼ tsp
10	peppercorns	10
2 tbsp	virgin olive oil	2 tbsp

Put the onion, lemon juice and peel, parsley, thyme, coriander, cumin, salt and peppercorns in a deep, non-reactive frying pan. Pour in enough water to cover the onion by 2.5 cm (1 inch). Bring the liquid to the boil over high heat, reduce the heat to medium-low and simmer the liquid for 10 minutes. Raise the heat to medium-high, bring the liquid once again to the boil and add the cauliflower. Cook the florets, turning them occasionally, until they are tender but not soft – about 10 minutes. Remove the pan from the heat and let the cauliflower cool to room temperature in the liquid. Transfer it to a vegetable dish with a slotted spoon; dribble on the oil just before serving.

Braised Celery

Serves 8

Working time: about 20 minutes

Total time: about 1 hour and 20 minutes

Calories 40
Protein 2g
Cholesterol 0mg
Total fat 0g
Saturated fat 0g
Sodium 200mg

4	heads celery	4
1	large-sized sweet red pepper	1
1	large-sized sweet green pepper	1
275 g	carrots, peeled and thinly sliced	9 oz
1	large onion, finely chopped	1

60 cl	unsalted chicken stock	1 pint
¼ tsp	salt	¼ tsp
1 tsp	mixed dried herbs	1 tsp
	finely chopped parsley for garnish	

Trim the celery and cut each head down to about 15 cm (6 inches) long (use the trimmings for salad or soup). Remove any bruised or woody outer stalks, then cut each head in half crosswise. Wash well.

Slice the top off each pepper and remove the seeds. Wash the peppers well, and cut eight thick rings from each one. Slide one red and one green pepper ring on to each celery heart.

Scatter the sliced carrots and the chopped onion over the base of a wide shallow saucepan,

arrange the celery hearts neatly on top, and pour in the chicken stock. Add the salt and sprinkle with the herbs. Bring to the boil, reduce the heat, cover and simmer until the celery is very tender – 1 to 1½ hours.

Carefully lift the celery hearts on to serving dish, cover and keep warm. Boil the pan juices until they are reduced and slightly thickened, then pour them over the celery. Sprinkle with parsley and serve immediately.

Steamed Cauliflower with Tomato and Basil Sauce

Serves 6

Working
time: about
25 minutes

Total time:
about
1 hour and
10 minutes

Calories
100

Protein
5g

Cholesterol
5mg

Total fat
7g

Saturated fat
2g

Sodium
140mg

1	large cauliflower	1	2 tbsp	very finely shredded basil leaves	2 tbsp
1 tbsp	virgin olive oil	1 tbsp		freshly ground black pepper	
1	large onion, skinned and finely chopped	1	15 g	unsalted butter	$\frac{1}{2}$ oz
			45 g	fresh breadcrumbs	$1\frac{1}{2}$ oz
1 kg	ripe tomatoes, skinned, seeded and roughly chopped	2 lb	1 tbsp	finely cut chives	1 tbsp
2	garlic cloves, crushed	2	2 tbsp	finely chopped parsley	2 tbsp
$\frac{1}{4}$ tsp	salt	$\frac{1}{4}$ tsp	2 tsp	fresh thyme leaves	2 tsp
				fresh basil leaves for garnish	

Heat the oil in a large saucepan. Add the onion and cook gently until softened – about 5 minutes. Put the tomatoes, garlic, salt and basil in the pan with the onion and bring to the boil. Reduce the heat, partially cover the pan and cook gently until the tomatoes are very soft and the sauce has thickened – 45 minutes to 1 hour. Season with pepper.

Meanwhile, trim the large outer leaves from the cauliflower, and make a deep cross in the stalk. Wash the cauliflower well, then steam it

gently until tender – 20 to 25 minutes.

Just before the cauliflower is cooked, melt the butter in a frying pan. Add the breadcrumbs and cook over a gentle heat, stirring continuously, until the crumbs are golden-brown. Stir in the cut chives, chopped parsley and thyme leaves.

Place the cauliflower, whole or broken into florets, in a hot serving dish. Pour the tomato sauce over the cauliflower, and sprinkle with the buttered crumbs. Garnish with basil leaves and serve immediately.

Bulb Fennel with Tomatoes and Black Olives

Serves 4

Working time: about 15 minutes

Total time: about 45 minutes

Calories 85
Protein 2g
Cholesterol 0mg
Total fat 5g
Saturated fat 1g
Sodium 150mg

2	fennel bulbs, green stems removed, halved lengthwise and thinly sliced	**2**
1 tbsp	virgin olive oil	**1 tbsp**
1	onion, thinly sliced	**1**
2	tomatoes, skinned, seeded and coarsely chopped	**2**
45 g	small, whole black olives	**1½ oz**
10 g	fresh basil leaves, torn into small pieces, or ½ tsp dried thyme leaves	**⅓ oz**
	freshly ground black pepper	

Heat the oil in a large, heavy frying pan over low heat and cook the onion until translucent – 8 to 10 minutes. Add the bulb fennel and continue cooking, stirring occasionally, until the fennel is tender – about 10 minutes. Stir in the tomatoes and olives. Raise the heat to medium and cook until all the moisture has evaporated – 8 to 10 minutes more. Stir in the basil or thyme, with the pepper. Transfer the vegetables to a warmed dish and serve immediately.

Bok Choy and Ham Gratin

Serves 8

Working time: about 40 minutes

Total time: about 45 minutes

Calories
100

Protein
7g

Cholesterol
15mg

Total fat
9g

Saturated fat
6g

Sodium
205mg

1 kg	bok choy (Chinese chard), washed and cut into 7.5 cm (3 inch) lengths	**2 lb**
1½ tbsp	safflower oil	**1½ tbsp**
1	small onion, thinly sliced	**1**
1	shallot, finely chopped	**1**
¼ tsp	salt	**¼ tsp**
⅛ tsp	white pepper	**⅛ tsp**
2 tsp	flour	**2 tsp**
35 cl	milk	**12 fl oz**
60 g	Gruyère cheese, grated	**2 oz**
⅛ tsp	grated nutmeg	**⅛ tsp**
60 g	lean cooked ham, julienned	**2 oz**
1 tbsp	finely cut chives	**1 tbsp**

Finely chop the bok choy by hand or in a food processor. Set the bok choy aside.

In a large, heavy-bottomed frying pan, heat 1 tablespoon of the oil over medium-high heat. Add the onion and shallot and sauté them, stirring frequently, until they are just translucent – about 5 minutes. Add the bok choy, salt and pepper, and cook until the bok choy stems are slightly limp – about 5 minutes more. Remove the pan from the heat, drain off any excess liquid and set the mixture aside.

Preheat the grill. In a small bowl, whisk together the flour and the remaining oil to form a paste. Pour the milk into a small saucepan and heat it over medium heat until the surface barely trembles. Whisk the flour paste into the milk until a smooth mixture results. Whisk in the cheese and nutmeg, blend well, then stir in about three quarters of the ham.

Put the bok choy mixture in a shallow fireproof dish, pour the cheese sauce over it, and stir well to combine. Arrange the remaining ham decoratively on top. Grill the dish until the surface has browned – 2 to 3 minutes. Sprinkle with the chives; serve at once.

Broccoli with Red Pepper Sauce

Serves 4

Working
(and total)
time: about
15 minutes

Calories
70
Protein
4g
Cholesterol
0mg
Total fat
4g
Saturated fat
1g
Sodium
160mg

500 g	broccoli, stalks trimmed to 5 cm (2 inches)	**1 lb**	**1½ tsp**	white wine vinegar	**1½ tsp**	
1 tbsp	virgin olive oil	**1 tbsp**	**1 tbsp**	chopped fresh tarragon, or 1 tsp dried tarragon	**1 tbsp**	
1	garlic clove, crushed	**1**	**1 tsp**	prepared horseradish	**1 tsp**	
2	sweet red peppers, seeded, deribbed and coarsely chopped	**2**	**¼ tsp**	salt	**¼ tsp**	
12.5 cl	unsalted chicken or vegetable stock	**4 fl oz**	**⅛ tsp**	ground white pepper	**⅛ tsp**	

Pour enough water into a saucepan to fill it 2.5 cm (1 inch) deep. Set a vegetable steamer in the pan and bring the water to the boil. Put the broccolli in the steamer, cover the pan tightly, and steam the broccoli until it is tender but still crisp – about 7 minutes.

While the broccoli is steaming, make the red pepper sauce. Heat the oil in a heavy frying pan over medium heat. Cook the garlic for 1 minute, then add the peppers and cook until they are soft – about 2 minutes. Pour in the stock and vinegar, then stir in the tarragon, horseradish, salt and pepper. As soon as the mixture reaches a simmer, remove it from the heat. Purée the mixture in a food processor or blender for about 2 minutes. Transfer the broccoli to a serving dish and strain the sauce over it. Serve immediately.

Mushrooms in Red Wine

Serves 4
Working time: about 20 minutes
Total time: about 45 minutes

Calories	170
Protein	4g
Cholesterol	0mg
Total fat	7g
Saturated fat	1g
Sodium	155mg

500 g	button mushrooms, stems trimmed and caps wiped clean	**1 lb**	**¼ tsp**	salt	**¼ tsp**
¼ litre	red wine	**8 fl oz**	**8**	garlic cloves, unpeeled	**8**
2 tbsp	virgin olive oil	**2 tbsp**	**1**	bunch spring onions, white bottoms sliced, green tops finely chopped	**1**
2–3	fresh thyme or rosemary sprigs, or 1 tsp dried thyme or rosemary leaves	**2–3**	**2 tsp**	finely chopped fresh rosemary freshly ground black pepper	**2 tsp**

In a large saucepan, combine the wine, oil, thyme or rosemary sprigs, salt and ¼ litre (8 fl oz) of water. Bring the mixture to the boil over high heat. Reduce the heat to medium, add the garlic cloves and simmer the liquid for 10 minutes. Stir in the mushrooms and the white spring onion slices. Simmer the vegetables, partially covered, until the mushrooms feel soft when pierced with the tip of a sharp knife – about 10 minutes.

With a slotted spoon, transfer the vegetables to a serving bowl. Discard the thyme or rosemary sprigs, and boil the cooking liquid until it is reduced to about 17.5 cl (6 fl oz) – 10 to 12 minutes. Pour it over the vegetables and stir in the spring onion tops. Sprinkle the vegetables with the chopped rosemary and the pepper, and mix well. Serve the mushrooms warm or well chilled.

Editor's Note: Preparing this dish a day or two ahead of time will intensify its flavour and impart a deep reddish hue to the mushrooms.

Ragout of Mushrooms with Madeira

Serves 4

Working time: about 30 minutes

Total time: about 1 hour and 30 minutes

Calories 135
Protein 5g
Cholesterol 0mg
Total fat 4g
Saturated fat 0g
Sodium 155mg

500 g	fresh mushrooms, wiped clean, stemmed and quartered	**1 lb**
30 g	dried shiitake mushrooms, soaked for 1 hour in warm water	**1 oz**
1 tbsp	safflower oil	**1 tbsp**
1	shallot, finely chopped	**1**
1	garlic clove, finely chopped	**1**
12.5 cl	Madeira or sherry	**4 fl oz**
2	tomatoes, skinned, seeded and chopped	**2**
½ tsp	dried thyme leaves	**½ tsp**
¼ tsp	salt	**¼ tsp**
	freshly ground black pepper	
1 tsp	cornflour, mixed with 1 tbsp of the mushroom-soaking liquid	**1 tsp**
1 tbsp	chopped parsley	**1 tbsp**

Squeeze the excess moisture from the shiitake mushrooms and finely chop them. Heat the oil in a large, heavy frying pan over medium-high heat. Sauté the fresh mushrooms for 1 minute, then add the shallot and cook, stirring, for 30 seconds longer. Add the shiitake mushrooms and garlic, and cook for 1 minute. Pour in the madeira or sherry, then stir in the tomatoes, thyme, salt and pepper. Cook until the mushrooms have softened – 3 to 4 minutes. Stir in the cornflour, and cook the ragout until it is slightly thickened – 1 to 2 minutes. Transfer the ragout to a serving dish and sprinkle with the chopped parsley.

Editor's Note: Although shiitake mushrooms are called for here, any dried wild mushroom – such as morels or ceps – may be used instead.

Stuffed Mushrooms with Goat Cheese and Spinach

Serves 6

Working time: about 30 minutes

Total time: about 1 hour and 15 minutes

Calories 85

Protein 3g

Cholesterol 12mg

Total fat 6g

Saturated fat 3g

Sodium 110mg

18	large mushrooms, wiped clean	18	2	garlic cloves, finely chopped	2
6 cl	dry white wine	2 fl oz	1 tbsp	virgin olive oil	1 tbsp
45 g	shallots, chopped	1½ oz	250 g	spinach, stems removed, leaves	8 oz
1 tsp	fresh thyme, or ¼ tsp dried thyme	1 tsp		washed, drained, squeezed dry	
1 tbsp	fresh lime or lemon juice	1 tbsp		and coarsely chopped	
15 g	unsalted butter	½ oz		freshly ground black pepper	
¼ tsp	salt	¼ tsp	90 g	mild goat cheese	3 oz

Carefully pull out the mushroom stems and chop them finely. Set the mushroom caps aside.

Preheat the oven to 180°C (350°F or Mark 4). In a frying pan, heat the wine, 8 cl (2 fl oz) of water, 2 tbsp of the shallots and the thyme over medium heat. Bring to the boil and cook for about 3 mins. Add the mushroom caps, bottoms facing up, and sprinkle with the lime or lemon juice. Cover and cook until shrunk by a third – 6 to 8 minutes. Remove from the heat. Take the caps out of the pan one at a time, tilting them to let any juices run back into the pan. Put on a baking sheet, bottoms down, to drain.

Return to the stove, reheat over medium heat. Add the mushroom stems, butter and half the salt; cook, stirring, until all the liquid is absorbed – 6 to 8 minutes. Transfer the stems to a bowl.

Wash the pan and return it to the stove. Add the oil and heat it over high heat. Stir in remaining shallots and the garlic. Place the spinach on top and sprinkle with the remaining salt. Cook, stirring, until all the liquid has evaporated – about 4 mins. Transfer to the bowl containing the mushroom stems, and sprinkle with pepper. Stir. Break the cheese into small pieces into the bowl, then fold it in.

Mound the spinach-and-cheese mixture into the mushroom caps. Place on a baking dish, and bake until they are browned on top and heated through – about 20 minutes. Serve warm.

Kohlrabies with Dill, Yogurt and Soured Cream

Serves 4		Calories 195
Working time: about 30 minutes		Protein 7g
		Cholesterol 10mg
Total time: about 1 hour and 30 minutes		Total fat 10g
		Saturated fat 4g
		Sodium 230mg

4	kohlrabies (about 1 kg/2 lb), leaves and stems removed	4
1 tbsp	safflower oil	1 tbsp
1	onion, finely chopped	1
60 g	celery, finely chopped	2 oz
2 tbsp	chopped fresh dill, or 2 tsp dried dill	2 tbsp
⅛ tsp	salt	⅛ tsp
	freshly ground black pepper	
45 g	bread cubes, from day-old French bread	1½ oz
12.5 cl	soured cream	4 fl oz
12.5 cl	plain low-fat yogurt	4 fl oz

Preheat the oven to 180°C (350°F or Mark 4). Place the kohlrabies in a lightly oiled baking dish and bake them until they feel tender when pierced with the tip of a sharp knife – 25 to 30 minutes.

Meanwhile, heat the oil in a large, heavy frying pan over medium heat. Add the chopped onion, celery and dill, and the salt and pepper, and cook until the vegetables are soft – 7 to 10 minutes. Remove the pan from the heat and set aside.

Slice the woody tops off the kohlrabies and discard them. Carefully hollow out each kohlrabi, leaving the walls about 5 mm (¼ inch) thick. Chop the scooped-out flesh and mix it with the vegetables in the pan. Stir in the bread cubes, soured cream and yogurt. Fill the kohlrabi shells with the mixture, then return them to the baking dish and bake them until they are heated through – 10 to 15 minutes.

Garnish each of the stuffed kohlrabies with a sprig of dill before serving.

Swiss Chard and Three-Onion Stew

Serves 8

Working
(and total)
time: about
1 hour

Calories
105

Protein
3g

Cholesterol
10mg

Total fat
5g

Saturated fat
2g

Sodium
145mg

1 kg	Swiss chard, washed, the stems cut into 1 cm (½ inch) pieces, the leaves coarsely shredded	**2 lb**
1	large carrot, peeled and cut into 5 mm (¼ inch) cubes	**1**
35 cl	unsalted chicken or vegetable stock	**12 fl oz**
350 g	potatoes, peeled and cut into 5 mm (¼ inch) cubes	**12 oz**
25 g	unsalted butter	**¾ oz**
1 tbsp	safflower oil	**1 tbsp**

1	red onion, coarsely chopped	**1**
2	small leeks, trimmed, cleaned and cut crosswise into 5 mm (¼ inch) slices	**2**
4	spring onions, trimmed and cut into 5 mm (¼ inch) slices	**4**
¼ tsp	salt	**¼ tsp**
½	lemon, juice only	**½**
	freshly ground black pepper	
1 tbsp	finely chopped parsley (optional)	**1 tbsp**

Pour enough water into a large saucepan to fill it about 1 cm (½ inch) deep. Add the carrot, cover and bring to the boil; Cook for 5 minutes. Add the chard stems and cook, covered, until tender – 3 to 5 minutes. Add the shredded chard leaves and cook, covered, for 3 minutes. Remove from the heat and leave uncovered to cool.

In a small saucepan, combine the stock and the potato cubes. Cover, bring to the boil and cook until the potatoes are very tender – about 10 minutes. Drain, reserving the stock, purée in a food mill or through a fine-meshed sieve. Stir the stock into the puréed potatoes and set aside.

In a large pan, heat the butter and oil over medium heat. Add the onion, leeks and spring onions, and toss to coat. Cover and cook, stirring occasionally, until vegetables are soft – about 5 mins. Stir in the chard mixture and the salt, re-cover, and cook, stirring occasionally for 10 mins.

Spoon the potato purée into the pan, mix, and cook until heated through. Stir in the lemon and pepper. Garnish with the parsley, serve at once.

Swiss Chard with Ham

Serves 6

Working time: about 20 minutes

Total time: about 30 minutes

Calories 45

Protein 4g

Cholesterol 5mg

Total fat 2g

Saturated fat 1g

Sodium 200mg

1 kg	Swiss chard, washed, the stems cut into 1 cm (½ inch) pieces, the leaves coarsely shredded	**2 lb**
1	onion, chopped	**1**
½ tsp	dried oregano	**½ tsp**
	freshly ground black pepper	
½ litre	unsalted chicken or vegetable stock	**16 fl oz**
60 g	smoked ham, shredded	**2 oz**
1 tbsp	white wine vinegar	**1 tbsp**

In a large saucepan with a tight-fitting lid, combine the chard stems, onion, oregano, pepper and stock. Bring the liquid to the boil, then reduce the heat to low, and simmer until the stems are tender – about 5 minutes. Remove the stems and onion from the stock with a slotted spoon and keep them warm.

Drop the chard leaves into the stock, cover the pan and return the stock to the boil. Cook the leaves until they are tender – about 3 minutes.

Without turning off the heat, use a slotted spoon to transfer the leaves to a heated platter. Scatter the stems and onion over the leaves and keep the dish warm.

Add the ham and vinegar to the boiling stock and cook until the liquid is reduced by half – about 5 minutes. Pour the stock mixture over the vegetables and serve at once.

Bean Sprout Sauté

Serves 4

Working
(and total)
time: about
20 minutes

Calories
100

Protein
2g

Cholesterol
0mg

Total fat
7g

Saturated fat
1g

Sodium
285mg

125 g	fresh bean sprouts	4 oz	125 g	medium carrot, peeled and	4 oz
2 tbsp	safflower oil	2 tbsp		shredded into long strips with a	
½ tsp	salt	½ tsp		grater	
¼ tsp	white pepper	¼ tsp	2	spring onions, trimmed, cut into	2
150 g	large yellow courgettes, halved	5 oz		5 cm (2 inch) pieces, sliced	
	lengthwise, seeded and shredded			lengthwise	
	into long strips with a grater		1 tbsp	cream sherry	1 tbsp

In a large, heavy frying pan, heat the oil over high heat. Sauté the bean sprouts for 1 minute. Sprinkle them with half the salt and pepper. Add the courgettes, carrot and spring onions, and sauté until the carrots are tender – about 2 minutes. Stir in the remaining salt and pepper. Remove the pan from the heat. Add the sherry and toss to incorporate. Serve the dish immediately.

Brussels Sprouts and Noodles with Dill

300 g	Brussels sprouts, quartered	10 oz
6 cl	plain low-fat yogurt	2 fl oz
6 cl	soured cream	2 fl oz
1 tbsp	chopped fresh dill, or 1 tsp dried dill	1 tbsp
¼ tsp	salt	¼ tsp
	freshly ground black pepper	
125 g	egg noodles	4 oz
15 g	butter	½ oz

Mix together the yogurt, soured cream, dill, salt and pepper in a small bowl and set aside.

Bring 3 litres (5½ pints) of water to the boil in a large saucepan. Boil the noodles in the water until they are cooked – about 5 minutes.

In the meantime, pour enough water into another saucepan to fill it 2.5 cm (1 inch) deep. Set a vegetable steamer in the pan and bring the water to the boil. Put the sprouts in the steamer, cover the saucepan tightly, and steam the sprouts until tender – about 5 minutes.

When the noodles are done, drain them and toss them with the butter. Stir in the sprouts and the yogurt and soured cream mixture. Transfer the sprouts and noodles to a warmed dish, and serve immediately.

Creamy Mustard Greens

Serves 6

Working time: about 35 minutes

Total time: about 55 minutes

Calories 125

Protein 5g

Cholesterol 15mg

Total fat 8g

Saturated fat 4g

Sodium 150mg

1 kg	mustard greens, washed, stemmed and coarsely chopped	2 lb
30 g	unsalted butter	1 oz
3 tbsp	chopped shallots	3 tbsp
1	garlic clove, finely chopped	1
¼ tsp	salt	¼ tsp

1 tbsp	safflower oil	1 tbsp
2 tbsp	flour	2 tbsp
40 cl	semi-skimmed milk	14 fl oz
¼ tsp	grated nutmeg	¼ tsp
	freshly ground black pepper	

In a large, heavy saucepan, melt the butter over medium heat. Add the shallots and garlic, and cook for 1 minute. Stir in the greens and the salt; cook, stirring frequently, until almost all the liquid has evaporated – about 15 minutes. Cover and set aside

In a small saucepan, heat the oil over medium heat. Add the flour and whisk until the mixture begins to bubble, then cook, stirring for 3 minutes more. Blend in the milk and cook, whisking constantly to prevent lumps, for about 3 minutes.

Reduce the heat to low. Add the nutmeg and pepper, continue to cook, whisking frequently, for 10 minutes more. Pour the sauce into the pan with the greens and toss to coat thoroughly. Serve immediately.

Editor's Note: Mustard greens, also known as green-in-snow or Chinese mustard, are not yet widely available though increasingly grown by home gardeners. Spinach or Swiss chard leaves could be used instead.

Stir-Fried Chinese Cabbage and Plantain

Serves 6

Working
(and total)
time: about
10 minutes

Calories
75
Protein
3g
Cholesterol
0mg
Total fat
2g
Saturated fat
0g
Sodium
5mg

1 kg	Chinese cabbage, shredded	**2 lb**
1 tbsp	safflower oil	**1 tbsp**
4	spring onions, sliced diagonally into 1 cm ($\frac{1}{2}$ inch) pieces	**4**

1	ripe plantain, sliced into thin rounds	**1**
$\frac{1}{2}$ tsp	crushed red pepper flakes	**$\frac{1}{2}$ tsp**
3 tbsp	rice vinegar or cider vinegar	**3 tbsp**

In a wok or a large, heavy-bottomed frying pan, heat the oil over high heat. Add the spring onion and plantain pieces and stir-fry for 1 minute. Add the cabbage and red pepper flakes; cook, stirring constantly, until the cabbage wilts – 1 to 2 minutes more. Pour in the vinegar and cook for 1 minute. Transfer the cabbage and plantain to a large dish and serve immediately.

Editor's Note: Although technically a fruit, plantains are used throughout Latin America and South-East Asia as a starchy vegetable. Plantains must be cooked before they can be eaten.

Marinated Red and Green Cabbage

Serves 8

Working time: about 30 minutes

Total time: about 4 hours and 30 minutes

Calories 120

Protein 2g

Cholesterol 0mg

Total fat 4g

Saturated fat 0g

Sodium 155mg

500 g	red cabbage, shredded	**1 lb**
500 g	green cabbage, shredded	**1 lb**
2	large carrots, grated	**2**
1	large red onion, very thinly sliced	**1**
2 tbsp	finely chopped fresh ginger root	**2 tbsp**
¼ litre	cider vinegar	**8 fl oz**
90 g	sultanas	**3 oz**
3 tbsp	honey	**3 tbsp**
2 tbsp	safflower oil	**2 tbsp**
½ tsp	salt	**½ tsp**
3	spring onions, trimmed and sliced	**3**
	freshly ground black pepper	

Pour enough water into a large saucepan to fill it about 2.5 cm (1 inch) deep. Place a vegetable steamer in the pan and bring the water to the boil. Put the cabbage and carrots in the steamer, cover the pot tightly, and steam the vegetables, stirring them once, for 5 minutes. Drain the vegetables well and transfer them to a mixing bowl. Add the onion, ginger and vinegar, and toss. Set the vegetables aside to marinate for at least 4 hours.

Squeeze the marinated vegetables a handful at a time over a saucepan to catch the juices; as you work, transfer the drained vegetables to a bowl. Boil the liquid over high heat until it has reduced to 12.5 cl (4 fl oz) – about 5 minutes. Add the sultanas and remove the pan from the heat. When the liquid has cooled, whisk in the honey, oil and salt. Pour the sauce over the drained vegetables, and stir in the spring onions and pepper. Serve chilled or at room temperature.

Cabbage Rolls with Barley and Tomatoes

Serves 8
as a
side dish,
4 as a
main course

Working
time: about
1 hour

Total time:
about
2 hours

Calories
120
Protein
4g
Cholesterol
5mg
Total fat
5g
Saturated fat
1g
Sodium
120mg

8	large green cabbage leaves	8
3	large tomatoes, cored	3
100 g	pearl barley, rinsed and drained	3½ oz
1½ tsp	dried oregano, or 3 tsp chopped fresh oregano	1½ tsp
2	garlic cloves, quartered	2
6 cl	red wine or cider vinegar	2 fl oz
2 tbsp	safflower oil	2 tbsp

1 tbsp	sugar	1 tbsp
150 g	courgettes, cut into 1 cm (½ inch) cubes	5 oz
¼ tsp	salt	¼ tsp
	freshly ground black pepper	
3	spring onions, trimmed, cut into 1 cm (½ inch) lengths	3
30 g	Parmesan cheese, freshly grated	1 oz

Bring 1 litre (1¾ pints) of water to the boil. Cut a cross on the bottom of each tomato. Immerse in the water. As soon as the skins begin to peel away, remove the tomatoes and set aside.

Add the barley and half the oregano to the boiling water; reduce to a simmer, cook, covered, until the water is absorbed. Transfer to a bowl.

While the barley cooks, skin, seed and chop the tomatoes. Place the tomatoes, garlic, vinegar, 1 tbsp of the oil and the sugar in a blender, and purée.

Bring 2 litres (3½ pints) of water to the boil. Add the cabbage and cook until limp. Drain. When cool, cut the core from the base of each leaf, set aside.

In a frying pan, heat the remaining oil over medium-high heat. Add the courgettes, the remaining oregano, salt and pepper. Sauté for 3 mins, then add the spring onions and cook for 30 secs more. Pour all but 12.5 cl (4 fl oz) of the puréed tomatoes into the pan; cook, stirring, until thickened. Add to the bowl with the barley. Sprinkle in the cheese and stir.

Put about ⅛ of the mixture at the stem end of a cabbage leaf. Roll up from stem to tip, turning in the sides after the first roll. Repeat for each.

Pour the reserved purée into a frying pan. Place the rolls, seam side down, in the pan. Cover and cook over low heat for 15 mins. Serve immediately.

Savoy Cabbage Stuffed with Chicken and Apple

Serves 4 as a main course

Working time: about 45 minutes

Total time: about 1 hour and 40 minutes

Calories 240
Protein 17g
Cholesterol 50mg
Total fat 11g
Saturated fat 4g
Sodium 190mg

One 2 kg	firm Savoy cabbage, outer leaves discarded	**One 4 lb**
1 tbsp	safflower oil	**1 tbsp**
300 g	onion, chopped	**10 oz**
1 tbsp	caraway seeds	**1 tbsp**
¼ tsp	salt	**¼ tsp**
	freshly ground black pepper	
6 tbsp	balsamic vinegar, or 4 tbsp red wine vinegar mixed with 2 tbsp water	**6 tbsp**

1 tsp	honey	**1 tsp**
25 g	unsalted butter	**¾ oz**
1	large dessert apple, cored and cut into 1 cm (½ inch) pieces	**1**
1 tbsp	fresh lemon juice	**1 tbsp**
250 g	chicken breast meat, cut into 1 cm (½ inch) cubes	**8 oz**
45 g	parsley sprigs	**1½ oz**

Hollow out the cabbage. Chop about 250 g (8 oz) of the scooped out leaves, and set aside.

In a frying pan, heat the oil over medium heat. Add the onion and caraway seeds, and cook for 2 mins. Stir in the chopped cabbage and the seasoning. Cook, stirring frequently, for 5 mins. Pour in 4 tbsps of the vinegar and the honey, and cook for 5 mins more. Transfer to a large bowl.

Melt the butter in the pan over medium-high heat. When the butter bubbles, add the apple and sauté, stirring frequently, for 3 mins. Add the lemon juice and chicken, and cook, stirring constantly, for 2 mins. Add the remaining vinegar, the parsley and some additional pepper, and sauté for 1 min more. Transfer to the bowl with the cabbage and mix well.

Fill the cabbage shell with the stuffing and replace the reserved cabbage lid. Set a rack in a large pan with a tight-fitting lid. Pour water into the pan about 2.5 cm (1 inch) deep. Place the stuffed cabbage, stem end down, on the rack, and bring to the boil. Cover, reduce the heat to medium low, and steam for 40 minutes. Remove the cabbage from the pan and cut it into serving wedges.

Spring Greens with Smoked Turkey

Serves 4

Working time: about 20 minutes

Total time: about 30 minutes

Calories 110

Protein 7g

Cholesterol 10mg

Total fat 5g

Saturated fat 1g

Sodium 230mg

600 g	spring greens, washed, stems and centre ribs removed, leaves coarsely chopped	**1¼ lb**	
1 tbsp	safflower oil	**1 tbsp**	
1	onion, thinly sliced	**1**	
1	apple, peeled, cored and grated	**1**	
⅛ tsp	salt	**⅛ tsp**	
	freshly ground black pepper		
15 cl	unsalted chicken or vegetable stock	**5 fl oz**	
90 g	smoked turkey meat	**3 oz**	

Heat the oil in a large, heavy frying pan over medium heat. Add the onion and cook until it turns translucent – about 5 minutes. Stir in the spring greens, apple, salt and pepper, and cook for 1 minute. Pour in the stock and simmer for 5 to 10 minutes, or until tender. Stir in the turkey and cook 5 minutes more. Serve immediately.

Editor's Note: Swiss chard leaves can be used instead of spring greens.

Chicory with Parsley Sauce

Serves 6

Working time: about 20 minutes

Total time: about 1 hour and 15 minutes

Calories 65

Protein 3g

Cholesterol 10mg

Total fat 3g

Saturated fat 2g

Sodium 95mg

12	small heads chicory	12
¼ litre	unsalted chicken stock	16 fl oz
1	bouquet garni, made with 6 parsley stems, 2 thyme sprigs and 1 bay leaf	1
6 cl	fresh lemon juice	2 fl oz
45 g	parsley leaves	1½ oz
8 cl	single cream	3 fl oz
⅛ tsp	salt	⅛ tsp
	freshly ground black pepper	

In a large non-reactive pan, bring the stock to the boil. Add the bouquet garni, cover the pan, and simmer the stock for 10 minutes. Add the lemon juice and chicory, and re-cover. Simmer until the chicory feels tender when pierced at the base with a sharp knife tip – 20 to 25 minutes. With a slotted spoon, transfer the chicory to a serving dish and keep it warm. Discard the bouquet garni, and boil the liquid until it is reduced to about 15 cl (¼ pint) – 15 to 20 minutes.

While the liquid is reducing, blanch the parsley leaves for 1 minute in boiling water and drain them. Purée the leaves in a food processor or blender. With the motor still running, slowly pour the reduced cooking liquid into the puréed parsley and blend well. Strain the sauce into a small saucepan set over low heat, and stir in the cream, salt and pepper. Drain off any liquid that may have collected in the serving dish, and pour the parsley sauce over the chicory. Serve immediately.

Braised Chicory with Apple

Serves 4

Working time: about 10 minutes

Total time: about 25 minutes

Calories 80

Protein 2g

Cholesterol 0mg

Total fat 4g

Saturated fat 0g

Sodium 85mg

500 g	chicory, cut into 2.5 cm (1 inch) slices	**1 lb**	
1	red apple, cut into eighths then into 1 cm ($\frac{1}{2}$ inch) slices	**1**	
1	lemon, juice only	**1**	
1 tbsp	safflower oil	**1 tbsp**	
$\frac{1}{8}$ tsp	salt	**$\frac{1}{8}$ tsp**	
	freshly ground black pepper		
2 tbsp	cider vinegar	**2 tbsp**	

Place the chicory, apple, lemon juice, oil, salt, pepper and 17.5 cl (6 fl oz) of water in a heavy frying pan. Cover and bring to the boil over high heat. Steam the chicory until it is tender – about 10 minutes. Uncover the pan and cook 1 or 2 minutes to evaporate the water. Reduce the heat to medium and cook until the chicory is browned – about 5 minutes. Pour the vinegar over the chicory, stir well and remove the pan from the heat. Transfer the chicory to a vegetable dish and serve.

Watercress Timbale with Sweetcorn and Pimiento

Serves 4

Working
time: about
25 minutes

Total time:
about
45 minutes

Calories
65

Protein
4g

Cholesterol
70mg

Total fat
2g

Saturated fat
1g

Sodium
170mg

2	bunches watercress, washed, thick ends of stems cut off	2
175 g	fresh sweetcorn kernels (about 1 large ear), or 175 g (6 oz) frozen sweetcorn kernels, thawed	6 oz
1	egg	1

8 cl	skimmed milk	3 fl oz
⅛ tsp	grated nutmeg	⅛ tsp
¼ tsp	salt	¼ tsp
¼ tsp	white pepper	¼ tsp
30 g	finely diced pimiento	1 oz

Place the watercress, with water still clinging to it, in a saucepan. Cover the pan and steam the watercress over medium heat until it is slightly wilted – about 1 minute. Plunge into cold water to arrest the cooking. When the watercress is cool, drain it and use your hands to squeeze out any excess liquid. Set the watercress aside.

Pour enough water into a saucepan to fill it about 2.5 cm (1 inch) deep. Set a vegetable steamer in the pan and bring the water to the boil. Put the sweetcorn in the steamer, cover the pan, and steam the sweetcorn until it is tender – about 4 minutes. Set aside.

Preheat the oven to 170°C (325°F or Mark 3). Place the watercress, egg, milk, nutmeg, salt and pepper in a food processor or a blender, and

process for about 5 minutes, stopping a few times to scrape down the sides. Transfer the purée to a bowl and mix in the sweetcorn.

Lightly butter the inside of four 175 g (6 oz) ramekins. Distribute the pimiento pieces evenly among the ramekins, then fill the ramekins with the purée mixture. Put the ramekins in a shallow ovenproof baking dish and pour enough boiling water into the dish to come half way up the sides of the ramekins. Bake until the timbales are nearly firm in the centre – about 20 minutes.

Allow the timbales to cool slightly, then wrap the bottom of each ramekin against a hard surface and invert the timbales on to serving plates. Serve the watercress timbales warm.

Kale Gratin with Ricotta and Parmesan Cheese

Serves 10		
Working time: about 40 minutes		
Total time: about 1 hour and 15 minutes		

Calories 130		
Protein 7g		
Cholesterol 5mg		
Total fat 4g		
Saturated fat 1g		
Sodium 165mg		

1.5 kg	kale, washed, stems removed	**3 lb**
¼ litre	unsalted chicken or vegetable stock	**8 fl oz**
1	onion, chopped	**1**
90 g	long-grain rice	**3 oz**
1 tbsp	chopped fresh thyme, or 1 tsp dried thyme	**1 tbsp**
125 g	low-fat ricotta	**4 oz**
5 tbsp	freshly grated Parmesan cheese	**5 tbsp**
¼ tsp	grated nutmeg	**¼ tsp**
¼ tsp	salt	**¼ tsp**
	freshly ground black pepper	
15 g	fresh white breadcrumbs	**½ oz**
1 tbsp	virgin olive oil	**1 tbsp**

Pour the stock into a small saucepan, add the onion and bring the liquid to the boil over high heat. Add the rice and thyme. Reduce the heat to medium low, cover the pan, and simmer the rice until it is tender – about 15 minutes.

Preheat the oven to 200° C (400°F or Mark 6).

Meanwhile, put the kale in a large saucepan, cover the pan tightly and cook the kale over medium-high heat until it wilts – 3 to 4 minutes. (The water clinging to the leaves provides enough moisture.) Drain the kale and coarsely chop it. Combine the kale with the rice, ricotta,

4 tablespoons of the Parmesan cheese, the nutmeg, salt and pepper.

Put the mixture into a lightly oiled 1½ litre (2½ pint) gratin dish. Sprinkle on the breadcrumbs and the remaining Parmesan cheese. Dribble the olive oil over the top and bake in the upper third of the oven until the juices begin bubbling – about 30 minutes. Remove the gratin from the oven and turn on the grill. Place the gratin under the grill to brown – about 5 minutes. Serve immediately.

Vegetable-Stuffed Cos Rolls

Serves 6		
Working time: about 1 hour		
Total time: about 1 hour and 10 minutes		

Calories 95		
Protein 4g		
Cholesterol 0mg		
Total fat 5g		
Saturated fat 1g		
Sodium 150mg		

12	large cos lettuce leaves	**12**	**2**	carrots, peeled and shredded into long strips	**2**
1	cucumber, peeled, halved lengthwise, seeded and shredded into long strips	**1**	**8**	spring onions, green tops removed, white bottoms thinly sliced lengthwise	**8**
1 tsp	low-sodium soy sauce, or naturally fermented shoyu	**1 tsp**	**1**	garlic clove, finely chopped	**1**
¼ litre	unsalted chicken or vegetable stock	**8 fl oz**	**¼ tsp**	salt freshly ground black pepper	**¼ tsp**
1 tbsp	safflower oil	**1 tbsp**	**150 g**	shelled peas, blanched for 1 minute and drained, or thawed frozen peas	**5 oz**
500 g	yellow squash or courgettes, halved lengthwise, seeded and shredded into long strips	**1 lb**	**1 tbsp**	dark sesame oil	**1 tbsp**

Put the cucumber in a bowl and toss with the soy sauce. Set aside to marinate. Place the lettuce leaves in a large pan and pour 12.5 cl (4 fl oz) of the stock over them. Place foil directly over the leaves and cover the pan. Bring to the boil, reduce the heat to medium-low, and steam until wilted – about 7 minutes. Drain on paper towels.

Squeeze the liquid from the cucumber. In a heavy frying pan, heat the safflower oil over high heat. Add the carrots and sauté, stirring constantly, for 1 min. Add the cucumber, squash,

spring onions, garlic, seasoning; sauté, stirring constantly, for 5 mins more. Transfer to a bowl and stir in the peas and sesame oil.

Cut out the thickest part of the lettuce stem. Overlap the edges and roll up the mixture in the leaves.

Pour the remaining 12.5cl (4 fl oz) of stock into a frying pan. Arrange the rolls in the pan, seam sides down; cover, cook over low heat until heated – about 10 mins. Remove from the pan and serve immediately.

Parsley with Burghul and Orange

Serves 6

Working time: about 45 minutes

Total time: about 1 hour

Calories 140
Protein 4g
Cholesterol 0mg
Total fat 5g
Saturated fat 0g
Sodium 70mg

225 g	parsley leaves	**7½ oz**	
2 tbsp	safflower oil	**2 tbsp**	
90 g	finely chopped onion	**3 oz**	
90 g	burghul	**3 oz**	
⅛ tsp	salt	**⅛ tsp**	
17.5 cl	fresh orange juice	**6 fl oz**	
60 g	grated radish		**2 oz**
	freshly ground black pepper		
3 tbsp	rice vinegar		**3 tbsp**
1	orange, peeled and segmented, the pith and membrane removed		**1**

Heat 1 tablespoon of the oil in a saucepan over medium heat. Add the onion and cook it, stirring once, for 2 minutes. Add the burghul and cook the mixture, stirring frequently, for 5 minutes more.

Stir in the salt, orange juice and 6 cl (2 fl oz) of water, and raise the heat to medium-high. When the mixture starts to simmer, reduce the heat to low; partially cover the pan, leaving a 2.5 cm(1 inch) opening to vent the steam. Cook, stirring occasionally, until the burghul has absorbed all the liquid – 15 to 20 minutes. Transfer the burghul mixture to a bowl, fluff it up with a fork, and refrigerate it.

While the burghul is cooking, pour enough water into a saucepan to fill it about 2.5 cm (1 inch) deep. Set a vegetable steamer in the pan and bring the water to the boil. Put the parsley in the steamer, cover the pan tightly, and steam until it turns a brighter green and is partially wilted – about 3 minutes. Immediately transfer to a large bowl and refrigerate.

When the burghul and the parsley have cooled, combine them. Then add the radish and the pepper, and toss well. In a small bowl, whisk together the remaining oil and the vinegar; dribble this liquid over the parsley and burghul. Add the orange segments and toss lightly. Transfer the mixture to a serving dish and serve it cool.

Vine Leaves Stuffed with Couscous

Serves 6

Working time: about 45 minutes

Total time: about 1 hour and 15 minutes

Calories 160

Protein 8g

Cholesterol 10mg

Total fat 7g

Saturated fat 1g

Sodium 145mg

18	fresh vine leaves, cooked 5 minutes in boiling water and refreshed under cold running water, or preserved vine leaves, rinsed	18
175 g	couscous	6 oz
500 g	mushrooms, wiped clean, finely chopped	1 lb
2	lemons, juice only	2
1	small onion, finely chopped	1
3	spring onions, chopped	3
1 tbsp	chopped fresh thyme, or 1 tsp dried thyme	1 tbsp
30 g	toasted almonds, chopped	1 oz
1 tbsp	virgin olive oil	1 tbsp
¼ tsp	salt	¼ tsp
	freshly ground black pepper	
½ litre	unsalted chicken or vegetable stock	16 fl oz
1	lemon, sliced	1

Place the couscous in a bowl and pour 30 cl (½ pint) of boiling water over it. Stir with a fork and let stand until the water is absorbed – about 10 minutes.

Place the mushrooms, half the lemon juice, the onion, spring onions and thyme in a saucepan; pour in enough water to cover. Bring the mixture to the boil over high heat, then reduce the heat to medium low and simmer for 10 minutes. Drain the mushrooms and discard the liquid. Preheat the oven to 200°C (400°F or Mark 6).

Combine the couscous, the mushroom mixture, almonds, oil, salt and pepper. Put a generous tablespoonful of filling close to the stem end of each leaf. Roll up the leaves, tucking in the edges to keep the couscous from spilling out, and pack them seam side down in a baking dish. Pour the stock into the dish and dribble the remaining lemon juice over the stuffed leaves. Cover tightly with aluminium foil and bake for 30 minutes. The stuffed leaves may be served warm or cold. Garnish the dish with the lemon slices just before serving.

Steamed Spinach with Water Chestnuts

Serves 6

Working time: about 20 minutes

Total time: about 30 minutes

Calories 65

Protein 6g

Cholesterol 0mg

Total fat 2g

Saturated fat 0g

Sodium 295mg

1 kg	spinach, washed, stems removed	**2 lb**
¼ tsp	Sichuan peppercorns, or ⅛ tsp freshly ground black pepper	**¼ tsp**
2 tbsp	low-sodium soy sauce, or naturally fermented shoyu	**2 tbsp**
1½ tsp	safflower oil	**1½ tsp**
½ tsp	dark sesame oil	**½ tsp**
1 tbsp	rice vinegar or cider vinegar	**1 tbsp**
¼ tsp	sugar	**¼ tsp**
125 g	water chestnuts, halved	**4 oz**

In a small, heavy frying pan, toast the peppercorns over medium heat for 3 minutes, shaking the pan frequently. Transfer the peppercorns to a work surface and crush them. In a small bowl, combine the soy sauce, oils, vinegar, pepper and sugar.

Place the spinach in a large pan, cover, and steam it over medium-high heat until it is wilted – about 2 minutes. (The water clinging to the leaves provides enough moisture.) Drain the spinach thoroughly and put it back in the pan. Stir in the water chestnuts and the soy sauce mixture, bring the liquid to the boil, and cook the spinach for 3 minutes. Transfer to a vegetable dish and serve.

Sautéed French Beans with Radishes and Fennel

500 g	French beans, topped and tailed	**1 lb**	**3**	spring onions, trimmed, thinly sliced	**3**
1 tbsp	virgin olive oil	**1 tbsp**	**¼ tsp**	salt	**¼ tsp**
1 tbsp	unsalted butter	**1 tbsp**		freshly ground black pepper	
2 tsp	fennel seeds	**2 tsp**	**1 tbsp**	fresh lime or lemon juice	**1 tbsp**
125 g	radishes, trimmed and sliced into 3 mm (⅛ inch) rounds	**4 oz**			

In a large saucepan, bring 2 litres (3½ pints) of water to a rapid boil. Add the beans and, after the water returns to the boil, cook them for 4 minutes. Remove them from the pan and refresh them under cold running water to preserve their colour. Drain the beans and set aside.

In a large, heavy frying pan, heat the oil and butter over medium-high heat. When the butter has melted, add the beans and the fennel seeds. Sauté for 3 minutes, stirring frequently. Add the radishes, spring onions, salt, pepper, and lime or lemon juice. Sauté, stirring constantly, until the beans are tender but crisp – about 3 minutes more. Serve immediately.

Chilled Beans with Yogurt and Mint

Serves 6

Working time: about 20 minutes

Total time: about 50 minutes

Calories 40
Protein 2g
Cholesterol 0mg
Total fat 1g
Saturated fat 0g
Sodium 100mg

500 g	French beans, topped and tailed	**1 lb**
¼ tsp	salt	**¼ tsp**
1½ tsp	dry mustaerd	**1½ tsp**
1 tbsp	fresh lime or lemon juice	**1 tbsp**
2 tbsp	chopped fresh mint	**2 tbsp**
1	small garlic clove, very finely chopped	**1**
½ tsp	sugar	**½ tsp**
	freshly ground black pepper	
8 cl	plain low-fat yogurt	**3 fl oz**
1	tomato, cut into wedges	**1**

Pour enough water into a large saucepan to fill it about 2.5 cm (1 inch) deep. Set a vegetable steamer in the pan and bring the water to the boil. Add the beans, cover the pan tightly, and steam the beans until they are tender – about 6 minutes. Remove the beans from the pan, and refresh them under cold running water to arrest their cooking and preserve their colour. When the beans are cool, drain them thoroughly and place them in a bowl. Sprinkle the salt over the beans and toss well.

In a bowl, stir together the dry mustard and the lime or lemon juice until a smooth paste is formed. Add the mint, garlic, sugar, pepper and yogurt, and blend well. Add the beans and toss to coat them. Refrigerate for at least 30 minutes. At serving time, garnish with the tomato wedges.

Broad Beans with Horseradish and Tomato

Serves 4

Working
(and total)
time: about
20 minutes

Calories
150
Protein
8g
Cholesterol
0mg
Total fat
3g
Saturated fat
0g
Sodium
140mg

300 g	fresh shelled, or frozen, broad beans	**10 oz**	
2 tsp	safflower oil	**2 tsp**	
¼ tsp	salt	**¼ tsp**	
	freshly ground black pepper		
2 tsp	horseradish	**2 tsp**	
1	small tomato, skinned, seeded and coarsely chopped	**1**	
2 tbsp	finely chopped fresh coriander	**2 tbsp**	

Bring 1 litre (1¾ pints) of water to the boil in a saucepan. Cook the beans in the water until barely tender – 8 to 10 minutes – then drain them and set them aside. (If you are using frozen beans, cook them in 6 cl/2 fl oz of boiling water for 6 to 10 minutes.)

In a large, heavy frying pan, heat the oil over medium-high heat. Add the beans and sauté them, stirring frequently, for 2 minutes. Sprinkle the beans with the salt and pepper. Stir in the horseradish and tomato, and sauté, stirring constantly, for 1 minute more. Transfer the mixture to a serving dish, sprinkle with the coriander and serve immediately.

Sweetcorn and Red Pepper Pancakes

Serves 8

Working time: about 30 minutes

Total time: about 45 minutes

Calories 110

Protein 4g

Cholesterol 35mg

Total fat 5g

Saturated fat 1g

Sodium 160mg

325 g	fresh sweetcorn kernels (about 2 large ears), or frozen sweetcorn, thawed	**11 oz**	**1 tsp**	fresh thyme, or ¼ tsp dried thyme freshly ground black pepper	**1 tsp**
1	egg yolk	**1**	**150 g**	sweet red pepper, seeded, deribbed, and finely chopped	**5 oz**
30 g	cornmeal	**1 oz**	**4**	egg whites	**4**
30 g	flour	**1 oz**	**8 tsp**	virgin olive oil	**8 tsp**

Chop half of the sweetcorn finely, by hand or in a blender. Place in a large bowl. Add the egg yolk, cornmeal, flour, thyme, salt and pepper to the bowl, and stir well. Add the sweet red pepper and the remaining kernels, and mix to incorporate them. Set this mixture aside.

In another bowl, beat the egg whites until soft peaks form. Fold half of the egg whites into the sweetcorn and red pepper mixture, and blend well. Then carefully fold in the remaining egg whites; the whites should not be completely incorporated.

Heat a large, heavy frying pan (preferably one with a non-stick surface) over medium heat. Put 2 teaspoons of the oil in the pan. When the oil is hot, drop tablespoonfuls of the sweetcorn and red pepper mixture into the pan, taking care not to let the edges touch. Cook until the bottom side of each pancake is golden-brown – about 3 minutes. Turn the pancakes carefully and cook them until the other side browns – about 3 minutes more. Remove the finished pancakes from the pan and keep them warm. Repeat the process, using 2 teaspoons of the oil each time, until all of the batter has been used. Serve immediately.

Editor's Note: If you are using frozen sweetcorn, whisk 1 teaspoon of sugar into the egg yolk.

Sautéed Cucumbers with Red Leaf Lettuce and Dill

Serves 4

Working (and total) time: about 20 minutes

Calories 55
Protein 1g
Cholesterol 15mg
Total fat 5g
Saturated fat 3g
Sodium 140mg

750 g	cucumbers, peeled, halved, seeded and sliced into 5 mm (¼ inch) pieces	1½ lb
15 g	unsalted butter	½ oz
2	shallots, finely chopped	2
¼ tsp	salt	¼ tsp
	white pepper	
4	leaves red or oak leaf lettuce, torn into large pieces	4
10 g	fresh dill, coarsely chopped	⅓ oz
1 tbsp	double cream	1 tbsp
	freshly ground black pepper	

In a large, heavy frying pan, melt the butter over medium-high heat. Add the shallots and sauté them, stirring constantly, until they turn translucent – about 1 minute. Stir in the cucumbers, sprinkle with the salt and white pepper, and cook them until they are slightly limp – about 3 minutes more. Add the lettuce and dill, and cook until the lettuce has wilted – about 1 minute. Pour in the cream and allow it to heat through – about 1 minute more. Sprinkle the vegetables with black pepper and serve immediately.

Cucumber Mousse with Gazpacho Sauce

Serves 8

Working time: about 45 minutes

Total time: about 2 hours and 30 minutes

Calories 70
Protein 5g
Cholesterol 5mg
Total fat 3g
Saturated fat 1g
Sodium 50mg

500 g	cucumbers, peeled, seeded and cut into 5 cm (2 inch) strips	**1 lb**
2 tbsp	powdered gelatine	**2 tbsp**
17.5 cl	unsalted chicken or vegetable stock	**6 fl oz**
¼ litre	plain low-fat yogurt	**8 fl oz**
1	lime, juice only	**1**
6	drops Tabasco sauce	**6**
2	spring onions, white bottoms chopped, green tops finely chopped and reserved for the sauce	**2**
1	hot green chili pepper, seeded	**1**
1 tbsp	chopped fresh coriander	**1 tbsp**
	Gazpacho Sauce	
1 kg	tomatoes, skinned, seeded, and finely chopped	**2 lb**
1 tbsp	virgin olive oil	**1 tbsp**
1	lime, juice only	**1**
4	drops Tabasco sauce	**4**
1	garlic clove, very finely chopped	**1**
1 tbsp	chopped fresh coriander	**1 tbsp**

In a small bowl, soften the gelatine in 6 cl (2 fl oz) of the stock until it is spongy. In a small saucepan, bring the remaining stock to the boil. Add the gelatine mixture to the stock and stir to dissolve the gelatine thoroughly. Set the gelatine mixture aside.

Purée the cucumbers, yogurt, lime juice, Tabasco sauce, spring onion bottoms, chili pepper and coriander in a food processor or blender. Add the gelatine mixture and blend. Pour the mixture into a 2 litre (3½ pint) mould

and chill until firm – at least 2 hours.

To make the sauce, mix the tomatoes, oil, lime juice, Tabasco sauce, garlic, reserved spring onion tops and coriander in a bowl. Refrigerate the sauce.

At serving time, run a blade along the edge of the mould to loosen the mousse. Set the mould in shallow hot water for 30 seconds, then invert the mousse on to a serving platter. Spoon the sauce around the mousse.

Aubergine Parmesan with Mint

Serves 8

Working time: about 20 minutes

Total time: about 1 hour and 45 minutes

Calories 65

Protein 4g

Cholesterol 5mg

Total fat 4g

Saturated fat 1g

Sodium 210mg

500 g	aubergines, cut into 1 cm (½ inch) cubes	**1 lb**
½ tsp	salt	**½ tsp**
2	tomatoes, skinned, seeded and chopped	**2**

1	garlic clove, finely chopped	**1**
1 tbsp	chopped fresh mint leaves	**1 tbsp**
1 tbsp	virgin olive oil	**1 tbsp**
60 g	low-fat mozzarella, freshly grated	**2 oz**
3 tbsp	freshly grated Parmesan cheese	**3 tbsp**

In a bowl, toss the aubergine with the salt. Place the aubergine in a colander, and weigh it down with a plate small enough to rest on top of the cubes. Let the aubergine drain for 30 minutes to eliminate its natural bitterness. Rinse the aubergine under cold running water to rid it of the salt, and drain it well.

Preheat the oven to 200°C (400°F or Mark 6). In a 23 by 33 cm (9 by 13 inch) rectangular baking dish, mix together the aubergine, tomatoes, garlic, mint and oil. Cover the dish with aluminium foil and bake until the aubergine is very tender – about 1 hour. Remove the dish from the oven and sprinkle the grated cheeses over the top. Re-cover the dish and bake until the cheeses have melted – about 5 minutes more. Serve immediately.

Steamed Aubergine with Soy and Ginger

Serves 8

Working time: about 15 minutes

Total time: about 40 minutes

Calories 25
Protein 2g
Cholesterol 0mg
Total fat 0g
Saturated fat 0g
Sodium 310mg

4	aubergines (about 125 g/4 oz each), cut in half lengthwise	4
4 tbsp	low-sodium soy sauce, or naturally fermented shoyu	4 tbsp
2 tsp	dry sherry	2 tsp
1 tsp	molasses	1 tsp
¼ tsp	dark sesame oil	¼ tsp
2 tsp	chopped fresh ginger root	2 tsp
2	garlic cloves, finely chopped	2
2	spring onions, cut diagonally into 2.5 cm (1 inch) long pieces, 3 mm (⅛ inch) thick	2

In a small bowl, combine the soy sauce, sherry, molasses, sesame oil, ginger and garlic. Set aside.

Score the skin of the aubergines with crisscross cuts 2.5 cm (1 inch) apart and 2 cm (¾ inch) deep. Place the halves, flat side down, on a heatproof plate, and pour the soy sauce mixture over them.

Pour enough water into a large saucepan to fill it 2.5 cm (1inch) deep, place two small bowls on the bottom and rest the plate on top of them. Cover the pan, bring the water to the boil over high heat, and steam the aubergines until tender – about 10 minutes. Remove the plate, scatter the spring onions on the aubergine and allow the aubergine to come to room temperature before serving

Mange-Tout in Basil Vinaigrette

Serves 8

Working time: about 15 minutes

Total time: about 20 minutes

Calories
115

Protein
4g

Cholesterol
0mg

Total fat
7g

Saturated fat
1g

Sodium
70mg

750 g	mange-tout, strings removed	**1½ lb**	**1 tbsp**	olive oil	**1 tbsp**
1	shallot, finely chopped	**1**	**1**	garlic clove, finely chopped	**1**
2 tbsp	fresh lime juice	**2tbsp**	**1 tbsp**	chopped fresh basil	**1 tbsp**
2 tbsp	balsamic vinegar, or 1 tbsp	**2tbsp**	**¼ tsp**	salt	**¼ tsp**
	red wine vinegar mixed with			freshly ground black pepper	
	½ tsp honey		**30 g**	whole almonds, toasted and	**1 oz**
2 tbsp	safflower oil	**2tbsp**		chopped	

To prepare the basil vinaigrette, combine the lime juice and the balsamic vinegar in a small bowl. Steep the shallot in the mixture for 5 minutes. Whisk in the safflower and olive oils, garlic, basil, salt and pepper.

Bring 3 litres (5 pints) of water to the boil in a saucepan. Add the mange-tout to the rapidly boiling water, stir them once, and cook for 30 seconds only. Drain the mange-tout and refresh them under cold running water until they are cool. Drain the mange-tout again and toss them with the vinaigrette and almonds. Serve cold.

Green Peas with Curried Mushrooms

Serves 6

Working time: about 30 minutes

Total time: about 45 minutes

Calories 70
Protein 5g
Cholesterol 5mg
Total fat 1g
Saturated fat 0g
Sodium 25mg

1 kg	peas, shelled, or 300 g (10 oz) frozen peas, thawed	**2 lb**
12.5 cl	unsalted chicken or vegetable stock	**4 fl oz**
175 g	mushrooms, wiped clean, thinly sliced	**6 oz**
1	onion, chopped	**1**
1 tsp	curry powder	**1 tsp**
12.5 cl	plain low-fat yogurt	**4 fl oz**

If you are using fresh peas, parboil them until they are barely tender – 3 to 4 minutes. Drain the peas and refresh them under cold running water. Drain them again and set aside. (Frozen peas do not need to be parboiled.)

In a saucepan, bring the chicken stock to the boil. Add the mushrooms, onion and curry powder. Lower the heat to medium, and cook until almost no liquid remains – 10 to 15 minutes. Add the peas, and cook them until they are warmed through – about 5 minutes. Stir in the yogurt and remove the pan from the heat. Transfer the vegetables to a warmed serving dish and serve immediately

Sugar Snap Peas and Red Grapes

Serves 4

Working (and total) time: about 25 minutes

Calories
80
Protein
3g
Cholesterol
5mg
Total fat
3g
Saturated fat
2g
Sodium
135mg

350 g	sugar snap peas, strings and stems removed	**12 oz**
15 g	unsalted butter	**½ oz**
1	shallot, finely chopped	**1**
¼ tsp	salt	**¼ tsp**

	freshly ground black pepper	
90 g	seedless red grapes, halved lengthwise	**3 oz**
1 tbsp	dry white wine	**1 tbsp**

Blanch the peas in boiling water for 2 minutes. Drain the peas, then refresh them under cold running water until cool. Drain them again and set them aside.

Heat the butter in a heavy frying pan over medium heat. Cook the shallot until soft – about 2 minutes. Add the peas, salt and pepper, and cook until the peas are heated through – 2 to 3 minutes. Add the grapes and wine, and cook until the wine has evaporated – about 1 minute. Serve immediately.

Editor's Note: Mange-tout work equally well in this recipe. Blanch them for 30 seconds only.

Sweet Pepper Sauté with Courgettes

Serves 6

Working time: about 35 minutes

Total time: about 40 minutes

Calories 40

Protein 1g

Cholesterol 0mg

Total fat 2g

Saturated fat 0g

Sodium 5mg

3	small sweet peppers, (one red, one green, one yellow) seeded, deribbed and cut into 2.5 cm (1 inch) squares	3
1	onion, coarsely chopped	1
6	garlic cloves, finely chopped	6
¼ tsp	crushed fennel seeds	¼ tsp
1 tbsp	virgin olive oil	1 tbsp
250 g	courgettes, trimmed and cut into 2.5 cm (1 inch) cubes	8 oz
⅛ tsp	saffron threads, soaked in 2 tbsp water	⅛ tsp
1 tbsp	anise-flavoured liquer (optional)	1 tbsp
4 tbsp	chopped fresh basil, or 4 tbsp chopped parsley plus 1 tsp dried basil	4 tbsp

In a large frying pan, bring ¼ litre (8 fl oz) of water to the boil over high heat. Add the onion, garlic and fennel seeds, and cook until the water has almost evaporated and the onions and garlic are soft – about 5 minutes. Add the oil, peppers, courgettes, saffron, the liqueur if you are using it, and 6 cl (2 fl oz) of water; continue to cook, stirring constantly, until all the vegetables are tender – about 5 minutes more. Stir in the fresh basil or the parsley and dried basil, and serve immediately.

Sweet Peppers with Herbed Rice

Serves 8

Working time: about 30 minutes

Total time: about 1 hour and 15 minutes

Calories 235

Protein 4g

Cholesterol 0mg

Total fat 5g

Saturated fat 1g

Sodium 15mg

6	red, yellow or green peppers, grilled and peeled	**6**
175 g	long-grain brown rice	**6 oz**
1	5 cm (2 inch) strip of lemon peel	**1**
2 tbsp	virgin olive oil	**2 tbsp**
1	onion, chopped	**1**
90 g	raisins, soaked in 12.5 cl (4 fl oz) dry white wine	**3 oz**
6 cl	unsalted chicken or vegetable stock	**2 fl oz**
1	lemon, juice only	**1**
3 tbsp	chopped parsley	**3 tbsp**
1 tsp	fresh thyme, or ¼ tsp dried thyme dried thyme	**1 tsp**
⅛ tsp	ground coriander	**⅛ tsp**

Bring 1 litre (1¾ pints) of water to the boil in a saucepan. Add the rice and the lemon peel. Simmer for 25 minutes over medium heat.

Remove the stems, ribs and seeds from the peeled peppers. Cut the peppers in half lengthwise. Set eight of the pepper halves aside as a garnish. Coarsely chop the remaining pepper halves and set them aside too. Preheat the oven to 200°C (400°F or Mark 6).

Heat 1 tablespoon of the oil in a large, heavy frying pan. Add the onion and cook until it is translucent – about 5 minutes. Add the raisins and wine, stock, and lemon juice. Bring to the boil and add the rice. Stir in the parsley, thyme, coriander and the chopped peppers. Transfer the rice mixture to a 1.5 litre (2½ pints) gratin dish. Mound up the rice slightly and arrange the pepper halves on top. Bake the dish for 20 minutes. Brush the peppers with the remaining oil before serving.

Red and Yellow Peppers with Rocket

Serves 4

Working time: about 45 minutes

Total time: about 1 hour and 15 minutes

Calories 65
Protein 3g
Cholesterol 0mg
Total fat 4g
Saturated fat 1g
Sodium 70mg

6	sweet red and yellow peppers, grilled and peeled	6
5	garlic cloves, unpeeled	5
1 tbsp	virgin olive oil	1 tbsp
1 tsp	balsamic vinegar or fresh lemon juice	1 tsp
⅛ tsp	salt	⅛ tsp
	freshly ground black pepper	
1	bunch rocket, leaves coarsely shredded (about 100 g/3 oz)	1

Preheat the oven to 180°C (350°F or Mark 4). Place the garlic cloves on a piece of aluminium foil, and sprinkle them with 1 teaspoon of the oil. Wrap them up in the foil, then bake until a clove can be pierced easily with a skewer – about 20 minutes.

Remove the stems, ribs and seeds from the peppers, working over a bowl to catch the juices. Strain the pepper juices and reserve them. Slice the peppers lengthwise into 1 cm (½ inch) wide strips.

Squeeze the softened garlic cloves out of their skins, purée them through a small strainer and add to the pepper juices. Stir in the vinegar or lemon juice, salt and pepper. Heat the remaining 2 teaspoons of oil in a large, heavy frying pan over medium-high heat. Add the rocket and cook it until it wilts – about 1 minute. Add the sliced peppers and stir in the garlic mixture; cook for 1 or 2 minutes more to reheat the peppers. Transfer the peppers and rocket to a serving platter. The dish may be eaten hot, cold or at room temperature.

Chayote Squash with Tarragon

Serves 4

Working time: about 15 minutes

Total time: about 25 minutes

Calories 75

Protein 1g

Cholesterol 0mg

Total fat 4g

Saturated fat 0g

Sodium 140mg

500 g	chayote squash, peeled, cut in half lengthwise, large seeds removed, thinly sliced	**1 lb**
1 tbsp	safflower oil	**1 tbsp**
1	large shallot, finely chopped	**1**
1	garlic clove, finely chopped	**1**
2 tbsp	chopped fresh tarragon, or 2 tsp dried tarragon	**2 tbsp**
¼ tsp	salt	**¼ tsp**
	freshly ground black pepper	
6 cl	unsalted chicken or vegetable stock	**2 fl oz**

Heat the oil in a large, heavy frying pan over medium heat. Cook the shallot and garlic for 1 minute only. Add the chayote slices, tarragon, salt and pepper, and toss to mix. Pour in the stock, reduce the heat to low and simmer until the chayote is tender but still crisp – 6 to 8 minutes. Transfer the squash to a warmed vegetable dish and serve immediately.

Editor's Note: Small, young chayote need not be peeled.

Pumpkin Purée with Orange and Ginger

Serves 6

Working time: about 30 minutes

Total time: about 1 hour and 30 minutes

Calories 110

Protein 2g

Cholesterol 10mg

Total fat 4g

Saturated fat 2g

Sodium 90mg

1.75 kg	pumpkin, or butternut squash, peeled, seeded and cut into 1 cm (½ inch) cubes	3½ lb
1½ tbsp	unsalted butter	1½ tbsp
¼ tsp	salt	¼ tsp

¼ litre	fresh orange juice with pulp	8 fl oz
1 tbsp	fresh lime juice	1 tbsp
1½ tbsp	finely chopped fresh ginger root	1½ tbsp

Melt the butter in a heavy frying pan over medium heat. Add the pumpkin and sprinkle with the salt. Cook for 20 minutes, stirring often. Add the juices and ginger. Continue cooking, stirring frequently, until the mixture has reached a dense, pasty consistency – about 35 minutes.

Purée the mixture in a food processor or blender, or through a sieve or food mill. Transfer to a piping bag fitted with a large star nozzle and pipe it into a vegetable dish. Alternatively, spoon the purée into the dish and decorate the surface with the back of a spoon.

Yellow Squash with Peppered Dill Sauce

Serves 6

Working time: about 40 minutes

Total time: about 45 minutes

Calories 55
Protein 2g
Cholesterol 10mg
Total fat 3g
Saturated fat 2g
Sodium 20mg

750 g	medium yellow squash or courgettes, halved lengthwise, seeded and cut into 1 cm (½ inch) pieces	**1½ lb**
25 g	unsalted butter	**¾ oz**
1½ tbsp	flour	**1½ tbsp**
¼ litre	unsalted chicken or vegetable stock	**8 fl oz**
45 g	fresh dill, coarsely chopped, plus 2 tbsp finely chopped fresh dill	**1½ oz**
2 tsp	fresh lemon juice	**2 tsp**
¼ tsp	cayenne pepper	**¼ tsp**
	white pepper	

Pour enough water into a saucepan to fill it about 2.5 cm (1 inch) deep. Set a vegetable steamer in the pan and bring the water to the boil. Put the squash in the steamer, cover the pan, and steam the squash until just tender – about 4 minutes. Remove the steamer and squash; pour out any water remaining in the pan. Return the squash to the pan and cover to keep it warm.

To prepare the sauce, melt the butter over medium heat in a small, heavy-bottomed saucepan. Add the flour and whisk until the mixture bubbles – about 1 minute. Stir in the stock and bring it to the boil, stirring constantly. Add the coarsely chopped dill and cook for 3 minutes more. Stir in 1 teaspoon of the lemon juice along with the cayenne pepper and white pepper. Strain the sauce over the squash in the pan, then stir in the remaining lemon juice and finely chopped dill. Add more white pepper and serve immediately.

Courgettes Sautéed with Shallots and Tomato Strips

Serves 6

Working (and total) time: about 35 minutes

Calories 75

Protein 2g

Cholesterol 0mg

Total fat 5g

Saturated fat 1g

Sodium 95mg

600 g	courgettes, ends trimmed	1¼ lb
1	large ripe tomato, skinned	1
2 tbsp	virgin olive oil	2 tbsp
¼ tsp	salt	¼ tsp
	freshly ground black pepper	

6	shallots, thinly sliced	6
2 tbsp	chopped parsley or fresh coriander	2 tbsp
1 tbsp	fresh lemon juice	1 tbsp

Put the skinned tomato stem end down on a cutting board. With a small, sharp knife, cut wide strips of flesh from the tomato, discarding the seeds and core. Slice the flesh into 5 mm (¼ inch) wide strips and set them aside.

Slice the courgettes into 5 cm (2 inch) rounds. Cut each round into six wedges.

Heat the oil in a large, heavy frying pan over medium-high heat. When the oil is hot, add the courgettes. Cook, stirring frequently, for 5 minutes. Sprinkle the courgettes with the salt and pepper; add the shallots and cook for another 3 minutes, stirring often. Add the tomato strips, the parsley or coriander, and the lemon juice. Cook for 4 minutes more to blend the flavours, and serve immediately.

Baked Courgettes with Coriander Pesto

Serves 6

Working time: about 15 minutes

Total time: about 40 minutes

Calories 65
Protein 3g
Cholesterol 5mg
Total fat 4g
Saturated fat 1g
Sodium 155mg

6	small courgettes (about 750 g/1½ lb)	**6**
25 g	fresh coriander, chopped	**¾ oz**
25 g	parsley, chopped	**¾ oz**
1 tbsp	pine-nuts	**1 tbsp**
1	garlic clove	**1**

¼ tsp	salt	**¼ tsp**
	freshly ground black pepper	
1 tbsp	virgin olive oil	**1 tbsp**
30 g	Parmesan cheese, freshly grated	**1 oz**

Preheat the oven to 160°C (325°F or Mark 3).

To make the pesto, combine the coriander, parsley, pine-nuts, garlic, salt and pepper in a food processor or blender. Purée until smooth – about 3 minutes. Add the oil and blend for 1 minute. Add the Parmesan and blend 2 minutes more.

Trim the courgettes and cut them in half lengthwise. Spread the pesto on the exposed flesh of one half of each courgette, and cover with the other half. Wrap the courgettes in aluminium foil. Bake them until just tender – 20 to 25 minutes.

Spring Vegetable Stir-Fry

Serves 4

Working time: about 30 minutes

Total time: about 30 minutes

Calories
170
Protein
7g
Cholesterol
0mg
Total fat
8g
Saturated fat
1g
Sodium
170mg

2 tbsp	virgin olive oil	**2 tbsp**
30 g	pine-nuts (optional)	**1 oz**
30 g	fresh ginger root, peeled and finely chopped	**1 oz**
2	garlic cloves, chopped	**2**
125 g	French beans, topped and tailed	**4 oz**
125 g	mange-tout, topped and tailed	**4 oz**
125 g	broccoli florets (optional)	**4 oz**
125 g	asparagus, trimmed, stems finely sliced diagonally	**4 oz**
125 g	carrots, peeled, thinly sliced diagonally	**4 oz**
½ each	small sweet red, green and yellow peppers, seeded and finely sliced	**½ each**
3	sticks celery, thinly sliced	**3**
3	spring onions, trimmed, thinly sliced diagonally	**3**
¼ tsp	salt	**¼ tsp**

Heat 1 tablespoon of the oil in a large frying pan. Add the pine-nuts and fry gently until they turn golden-brown. Remove them from the pan and set them aside.

Pour 1 tablespoon of oil into the pan and heat. Add the ginger and garlic and cook for 2 to 3 seconds, then add the beans and stir-fry for about 2 minutes. Add the mange-tout, stir-fry for 1 minute, then add the broccoli, asparagus and carrots, and stir-fry for 2 minutes more. Add the remaining oil, the peppers, celery, and spring onions, and stir-fry until the vegetables are just tender – 2 to 3 minutes. Season with the salt, and stir in the reserved pine-nuts.

Transfer to a hot serving dish and garnish, if liked, with finely sliced spring onions. Serve immediately.

Summer Vegetable Stew

Serves 10

Working time: about 40 minutes

Total time: about 1 hour

Calories 115

Protein 4g

Cholesterol 5mg

Total fat 6g

Saturated fat 1g

Sodium 145mg

3 tbsp	safflower oil	**3 tbsp**
8	small shallots, peeled	**8**
250 g	mushrooms, wiped, left whole if small, halved or quartered if large	**8 oz**
1	yellow squash or courgette, cut into 2.5 cm (1 inch) cubes	**1**
2	sticks celery, cut into 2.5 cm (1 inch) pieces	**2**
1	sweet red pepper, seeded, deribbed and cut into 2.5 cm (1 inch) wide strips	**1**
1	small aubergine, cut into 2.5 cm (1 inch) cubes	**1**
2	garlic cloves, finely chopped	**2**
2	medium tomatoes, skinned, seeded and chopped	**2**
12.5 cl	dry vermouth	**4 fl oz**
½ tsp	salt	**½ tsp**
	freshly ground black pepper	
1	small potato, peeled and grated	**1**
1	ear of sweetcorn, cut into 2.5 cm (1 inch) pieces	**1**
250 g	young carrots, peeled	**8 oz**
250 g	French beans, topped and tailed	**8 oz**
1	bay leaf	**1**
⅛ tsp	saffron threads, steeped in 6 cl (2 fl oz) hot water	**⅛ tsp**
2 tbsp	chopped fresh marjoram, or 2 tsp dried marjoram	**2 tbsp**
60 g	Parmesan cheese, freshly grated	**2 oz**

Heat 1 tbsp of the oil in a frying pan over high heat. Sauté the shallots until lightly coloured – about 1 min. Add the mushrooms, squash, celery and red pepper, and sauté for 2 mins, stirring frequently. Transfer to a bowl and set aside.

Heat the remaing oil in the pan over high heat; add the aubergine and sauté for 2 mins. Stir in the garlic and cook briefly – 15 seconds max.

Return the vegetables to the pan; add the tomatoes and vermouth. Cook until reduced – 5 mins. Season.

Add the potato, with the sweetcorn, carrots, beans, bay leaf and water to cover. Simmer, uncovered, until tender –25 to 30 mins. Stir in the saffron mixture and the marjoram. When serving, sprinkle with the Parmesan.

Vegetable Mosaic

Serves 10

Working time: about 45 minutes

Total time: about 2 hours

Calories
120

Protein
4g

Cholesterol
0mg

Total fat
6g

Saturated fat
1g

Sodium
195mg

850 g	large onions, thinly sliced	**1¾ lb**
2	fennel bulbs, stems removed and feathery tops reserved, bulbs halved lengthwise and thinly sliced	**2**
¾ tsp	salt	**¾ tsp**
	freshly ground black pepper	
1 tbsp	fresh rosemary, or ¾ tsp dried rosemary, crumbled	**1 tbsp**
6 cl	cider vinegar	**2 fl oz**
600 g	courgettes, cut diagonally into 5 mm (¼ inch) thick slices	**1¼ lb**
2	garlic cloves, finely chopped	**2**
2 tbsp	chopped fresh oregano, or 2 tsp dried oregano	**2 tbsp**
6	ripe plum tomatoes	**6**
600 g	small aubergines, halved length-wise into 1 cm (½ inch) thick slices	**1¼ lb**
4 tbsp	virgin olive oil	**4 tbsp**

Put the onions and fennel in a large casserole with ¼ tsp of salt, some pepper and ½ of the rosemary. Pour in the vinegar and 6 cl (2 fl oz) of water. Cook over medium heat, scraping the pan frequently to mix in any caramelized bits, until vegetables are well browned – 30 to 35 mins.

Prepare the other vegetables. Preheat the grill. Toss the courgette slices in a bowl with the garlic, ½ the oregano and ¼ tsp of the salt. Cut the tomatoes into slices 5 mm (¼ inch) thick. Put on a plate and sprinkle with some pepper and remaining salt. Put the aubergine slices on a baking sheet and brush with 1 tbsp of the oil. Grill them until they are very brown – about

8 mins. Turn the aubergine and brush with another tbsp of the oil. Grill the aubergine on the second side until they are brown – 6 to 7 mins. Preheat the oven to 190°C (375°F or Mark 5).

Spread the onions and fennel in the bottom of a baking dish. Arrange the aubergine, courgette and tomato on the onions. Dribble 1 tbsp of the oil over the vegetables and cover with foil.

Bake the vegetables for 25 mins. Remove the foil and dribble the remaining oil over the top. Continue to bake, uncovered, until soft – about 20 mins. Sprinkle with remaining rosemary and oregano, and bake for 10 mins more. Garnish the dish with the reserved fennel tops.

Stewed Tomatoes with Cubed Rye Bread

Serves 6

Working time: about 20 minutes

Total time: about 1 hour

Calories 115

Protein 3g

Cholesterol 0mg

Total fat 3g

Saturated fat 0g

Sodium 170mg

6	tomatoes, skinned, seeded and coarsely chopped	**6**
1 tbsp	virgin olive oil	**1 tbsp**
1	onion, finely chopped	**1**
2	sticks celery, finely chopped	**2**
2	garlic cloves, finely chopped	**2**
2 tbsp	chopped fresh basil, or 2 tsp dried basil plus 1½ tsp chopped parsley	**2 tbsp**
¼ tsp	salt	**¼ tsp**
	freshly ground black pepper	
2 tbsp	dark brown sugar	**2 tbsp**
30 g	dark rye bread, cubed	**1 oz**

Preheat the oven to 180°C (350°F or Mark 4). In a large, heavy frying pan, heat the oil over medium-low heat. Add the onion, celery, garlic, 1½ tablespoons of the basil (or 2 teaspoons of dried basil), salt and pepper. Stirring occasionally, cook the mixture until the celery is limp – about 4 minutes. Stir in the tomatoes and cook them, stirring occasionally until they have softened – about 5 minutes. Add the brown sugar and the bread cubes, and combine. Place the mixture in a shallow baking dish and bake until the top is nicely dry – 35 to 40 minutes. Serve garnished with the remaining fresh basil, if you are using it, or sprinkle the dish with the chopped parsley.

Aromatic Potatoes and Leeks

Serves 6

Working time: about 30 minutes

Total time: about 2 hours

Calories 205

Protein 5g

Cholesterol 5mg

Total fat 1g

Saturated fat 0g

Sodium 125mg

1.5 kg	potatoes, peeled and sliced into 5 mm (¼ inch) rounds	**3 lb**
¼ litre	unsalted chicken or vegetable stock	**16 fl oz**
3	leeks, trimmed, cleaned and cut into 5 mm (¼ inch) pieces	**3**
3	garlic cloves, finely chopped	**3**
1½ tsp	fresh rosemary, or ½ tsp dried rosemary	**1½ tsp**
½ tsp	chopped fresh savory, or ¼ tsp dried savory	**½ tsp**
1 tsp	fresh thyme, or ¼ tsp dried thyme	**1 tsp**
¼ tsp	salt	**¼ tsp**
	freshly ground black pepper	
1	lemon, juice only	**1**

Preheat the oven to 220°C (425°F or Mark 7). In a small saucepan, combine the stock, leeks and garlic; bring the liquid to the boil, lower the heat and simmer for 3 minutes. Strain, reserving both liquid and solids.

Combine the rosemary, savory, thyme, salt and pepper in a small bowl. Arrange one third of the potatoes in a layer in a baking dish. Spread half the leek mixture over the potatoes, then sprinkle with half the herb mixture. Arrange half the remaining potatoes in a second layer and top with the remaining leek and herb mixture. Add the rest of the potatoes in a final layer. Pour the lemon juice and the reserved stock over all.

Cover the dish with foil and bake it for 30 minutes. Uncover the dish and return it to the oven until the top turns crisp and golden – about 1 hour more.

Potato Swirls

Serves 8

Working time: about 20 minutes

Total time: about 1 hour and 30 minutes

Calories 75
Protein 3g
Cholesterol 5mg
Total fat 2g
Saturated fat 0g
Sodium 90mg

850 g	potatoes, scrubbed	**1¾ lb**	**¼ tsp**	salt	**¼ tsp**
1	garlic clove, finely chopped	**1**	**¼ tsp**	white pepper	**¼ tsp**
1 tbsp	virgin olive oil	**1 tbsp**	**12.5 cl**	plain low-fat yogurt	**4 fl oz**
2	egg whites, lightly beaten	**2**	**2 tbsp**	finely cut chives	**2 tbsp**
¼ tsp	grated nutmeg	**¼ tsp**			

Preheat the oven to 200°C (400°F or Mark 6). Prick the potatoes and bake them until they are tender – about 1 hour. When the potatoes are cool enough to handle, scoop out the flesh and work it through a food mill or a sieve to achieve a smooth purée. (Puréeing the potatoes in a food processor or blender would make them gluey.)

Combine the garlic and oil in a small saucepan over medium heat and cook for 1 or 2 minutes (this softens the garlic and mellows its flavour). Add the garlic and oil to the potatoes with the egg whites, nutmeg, salt and pepper. Transfer the mixture to a piping bag fitted with a large star nozzle. Pipe eight rounds about 5 cm (2 inches) in diameter on to an oiled baking sheet. Pipe a raised border on the edge of each round. (If you do not have a piping bag, form the potato mixture into eight mounds and make an indentation in the top of each with the back of a spoon.)

Bake the potato swirls until the edges are crisp and brown – 7 to 10 minutes. With a spatula, transfer the swirls to a serving platter or individual plates. Combine the yogurt and the cut chives in a small bowl, and spoon this mixture into the centre of each swirl. Serve the potato swirls hot.

Baked Potatoes Hungarian-Style

Serves 4

Working time: about 15 minutes

Total time: about 1 hour and 15 minutes

Calories 130

Protein 5g

Cholesterol 2mg

Total fat 1g

Saturated fat 0g

Sodium 170mg

4	medium potatoes, scrubbed	**4**
12.5 cl	unsalted chicken or vegetable stock	**4 fl oz**
1	onion, finely chopped	**1**
2	garlic cloves, finely chopped	**2**

1¼ tsp	paprika	**1¼ tsp**
12.5 cl	plain low-fat yogurt	**4 fl oz**
¼ tsp	salt	**¼ tsp**
	freshly ground black pepper	

Preheat the oven to 200°C (400°F or Mark 6). Prick the potatoes and bake them for 1 hour.

Near the end of the baking time, combine the stock, onion and garlic in a saucepan. Bring to the boil and cook until the onions are tender – about 5 minutes.

When the potatoes are done, cut a lengthwise slice off the top of each one. Hollow out each potato, forming shells about 5 mm (¼ inch) thick.

To prepare the stuffing, stir the scooped-out potato flesh into the onion mixture in the saucepan. Add 1¼ teaspoons of the paprika, 6 cl (2 fl oz) of the yogurt, the salt and pepper, and stir well. Work the mixture through a food mill or a sieve to achieve a smooth stuffing.

Loosely fill the potato shells with the stuffing and reheat them in the oven for 10 minutes. Just before serving the stuffed potatoes, top them with the remaining yogurt and sprinkle them with the remaining ¼ teaspoon of paprika.

Sweet Potato and Pear Mousse

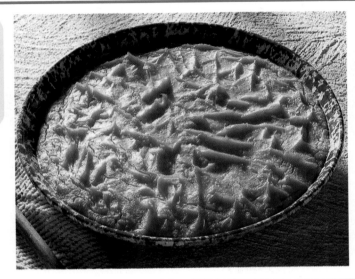

1 kg	sweet potatoes	2 lb
2	large ripe pears, peeled, cored and cut into 2.5 cm (1 inch) cubes	2
3 tbsp	fresh lemon juice	3 tbsp
¼ tsp	curry powder	¼ tsp
¼ tsp	cinnamon	¼ tsp
15 g	unsalted butter	½ oz
275 g	chopped onion	9 oz
¼ litre	apple juice	8 fl oz
	freshly ground black pepper	
1	egg yolk	1
2	egg whites	2

Preheat the oven to 230°C (450°F or Mark 8). Prick the sweet potatoes and bake them until they have begun to soften – about 30 minutes. Remove the sweet potatoes from the oven and set them aside to cool. Reduce the oven temperature to 180°C (350°F or Mark 4).

In a large bowl, combine the pears, lemon juice, curry powder and cinnamon. When the sweet potatoes are cool enough to handle, cut them in half lengthwise. Peel the sweet potatoes, cut them into 2.5 cm (1 inch) cubes and add them to the bowl.

Heat the butter in a large, heavy frying pan over medium heat. Add the onion and cook it for 5 minutes, then stir in the apple juice, the sweet potato mixture and freshly ground black pepper. Cover the pan, leaving the lid slightly ajar, and cook the mixture for 15 minutes, stirring occasionally.

Transfer the contents of the pan to a food processor or blender. Purée the mixture, stopping two or three times to scrape down the sides. Transfer the purée to a bowl and stir in the egg yolk.

In a separate metal bowl, beat the egg whites until soft peaks form. Fold the beaten whites into the purée and pour the mixture into a lightly buttered 2 litre (3½ pint) gratin dish. Bake the mousse for 30 minutes. Serve the mousse immediately.

Scorzonera with Mixed Herbs

Serves 6

Working time: about 30 minutes

Total time: about 45 minutes

Calories 100

Protein 3g

Cholesterol 5mg

Total fat 2g

Saturated fat 1g

Sodium 190mg

750 g	scorzonera, scrubbed well	**1½ lb**
1	lemon juice only	**1**
30 g	flour	**1 oz**
½ tsp	salt	**½ tsp**
15 g	unsalted butter	**½ oz**
⅛ tsp	white pepper	**⅛ tsp**

1 tsp	chopped fresh thyme, or ¼ tsp dried thyme	**1 tsp**
1 tsp	chopped fresh marjoram, or ¼ tsp dried marjoram	**1 tsp**
1 tsp	finely cut chives	**1 tsp**
1 tsp	chopped parsley	**1 tsp**

To keep the scorzonera from discolouring, add the lemon juice to 2 litres (3½ pints) of very cold water. Peel the scorzonera with a vegetable peeler and cut them in half, dropping the pieces into the acidulated water as you work.

To cook the scorzonera, first prepare a *blanc* – a cooking liquid that keeps the vegetable from discolouring. Put the flour in a large non-reactive saucepan and stir in just enough of the acidulated water to make a paste; then stir in the rest of the water. Add the scorzonera and half the salt. Bring to the boil, stirring occasionally to keep the flour from forming lumps. Cook until tender – 10 to 12 minutes – and drain.

Melt the butter in a large, heavy frying pan over high heat. Add the scorzonera, and shake the pan back and forth over the heat to coat it with the butter – about 1 minute. Then season with the remaining salt, the pepper and the herbs. Cook for 30 seconds longer to release the herbs' bouquet. Serve immediately.

Editor's Note: Scorzonera is similar to the lighter-skinned salsify, which can be used instead in this recipe.

Vegetable Couscous

Serves 8
as a
main dish

Working
time: about
35 minutes

Total time:
about
1 hour

Calories
215

Protein
9g

Cholesterol
5mg

Total fat
5g

Saturated fat
2g

Sodium
345mg

4	tomatoes, skinned and seeded	4	350 g	courgettes, quartered lengthwise and cut into 5 cm (2 inch) lengths	12 oz
1.25 litres	unsalted chicken or vegetable stock	2 pints	1	medium turnip, peeled and cut into 2 cm (¾ inch) pieces	1
2	medium onions, peeled and cut into 2.5 cm (1 inch) pieces	2	½	hot green chili pepper, seeded, rinsed and finely chopped	½
2	carrots, peeled and cut diagonally into 1 cm (½ inch) ovals	2	30 g	unsalted butter	1 oz
¾ tsp	salt	¾ tsp	350 g	couscous	12 oz
25 g	fresh coriander or parsley leaves	¾ oz			

Chop half of the tomatoes into 2.5 cm (1 inch) pieces and set them aside. Purée the remaining tomatoes in a processor or blender. Transfer the purée to a large pan, and add ½ litre (16 fl oz) of the stock. Heat the mixture over medium heat. Then add the onions, carrots, ¼ teaspoon of the salt and the coriander or parsley. Simmer, stirring occasionally, for 10 minutes.

Stir in the courgettes, turnip, the tomato pieces, chili pepper and ¼ teaspoon of the salt. Partially cover the pan, leaving a 2.5 cm (1 inch) opening to vent the steam, and cook the mixture

for 30 minutes more.

Meanwhile, pour the remaining stock into a large, heavy pan with tight-fitting lid. Stir in the butter and the remaining salt; bring the liquid to a rolling boil. Stir in the couscous and cook it stirring constantly, for 30 seconds. Remove from the heat, cover and let it stand for 7 minutes, then transfer it to a serving dish and fluff it with a fork.

To serve, divide the couscous among individual bowls. Spoon some vegetables and broth over each serving.

Leek Pie

Serves 6

Working time: about 40 minutes

Total time: about 1 hour

Calories 250
Protein 9g
Cholesterol 15mg
Total fat 8g
Saturated fat 3g
Sodium 145mg

1 kg	potatoes, peeled	2½ lb	1 tbsp	virgin olive oil	1 tbsp
4–5 tbsp	skimmed milk	4–5 tbsp	¼ tsp	salt	¼ tsp
75 g	Gruyère cheese, finely grated	2½ oz	2 tsp	mixed dried herbs	2 tsp
	freshly ground black pepper		30 cl	unsalted chicken stock or	½ pint
750 g	leeks, trimmed and washed	1½ lb		skimmed milk	
	thoroughly		15 g	unsalted butter	½ oz
1	large onion, thinly sliced	1	15 g	plain flour	½ oz

Cut the potatoes into quarters, then steam them until cooked through – about 25 to 30 minutes. Mash the cooked potatoes well, beat in the milk and cheese and season with pepper. Put the potatoes into a large piping bag fitted with a large star nozzle and pipe an attractive border round the inside edge of a fireproof dish.

Cut the leeks into 1 cm (½ inch) thick slices. Heat the oil in a large shallow saucepan, then add the leeks, onion, salt and herbs. Cover the pan with a tightly fitting lid and cook gently until the leeks are just tender, shaking the pan

frequently during cooking – 25 to 30 minutes. Strain the juices from the leeks and make them up to 30 cl (½ pint) with chicken stock or milk. Set the leeks aside.

Melt the butter in the saucepan, add the flour, and stir in the leek juices and stock or milk. Bring slowly to the boil, stirring all the time until the sauce thickens. Return the leeks to the pan, reduce the heat and simmer gently for 5 minutes.

Brown the piped potato border under a hot grill, then pour the leeks into the centre. Serve immediately.

Julienned Turnips in a Warm Vinaigrette

Serves 4

Working (and total) time: about 20 minutes

Calories
40

Protein
1g

Cholesterol
0mg

Total fat
1g

Saturated fat
0g

Sodium
95mg

350 g	turnips, peeled and julienned	**12 oz**	**½ tsp**	ground coriander	**½ tsp**
3 tbsp	fresh lime juice	**3 tbsp**	**⅛ tsp**	salt	**⅛ tsp**
1 tbsp	raspberry or red wine vinegar	**1 tbsp**		freshly ground black pepper	
1 tsp	virgin olive oil	**1 tsp**	**125 g**	courgettes, julienned	**4 oz**
½ tsp	honey	**½ tsp**	**30 g**	radishes, sliced	**1 oz**

To prepare the vinaigrette, combine the lime juice, vinegar, oil, honey, coriander, salt and pepper in a small saucepan. Warm the vinaigrette over low heat while you prepare the vegetables.

Pour enough water into a large saucepan to fill it about 2.5 cm (1 inch) deep. Set a vegetable steamer in the pan and bring the water to the boil. Add the turnips and steam them for about 1 minute. Then add the courgettes and radishes, and steam them until all of the vegetables are soft but not limp – about 1 minute more. Transfer the vegetables to a serving dish.

Bring the vinaigrette just to the boil and pour it over the vegetables. Toss well and serve at once.

Useful weights and measures

Weight Equivalents

Avoirdupois		Metric
1 ounce	=	28.35 grams
1 pound	=	254.6 grams
2.3 pounds	=	1 kilogram

Liquid Measurements

¹/₄ pint	=	1¹/₂ decilitres
¹/₂ pint	=	¹/₄ litre
scant 1 pint	=	¹/₂ litre
1³/₄ pints	=	1 litre
1 gallon	=	4.5 litres

Liquid Measures

1 pint	= 20 fl oz	= 32 tablespoons
¹/₂ pint	= 10 fl oz	= 16 tablespoons
¹/₄ pint	= 5 fl oz	= 8 tablespoons
¹/₈ pint	= 2¹/₂ fl oz	= 4 tablespoons
¹/₁₆ pint	= 1¹/₄ fl oz	= 2 tablespoons

Solid Measures

1 oz almonds, ground = 3³/₄ level tablespoons
1 oz breadcrumbs fresh = 7 level tablespoons
1 oz butter, lard = 2 level tablespoons
1 oz cheese, grated = 3¹/₂ level tablespoons
1 oz cocoa = 2³/₄ level tablespoons
1 oz desiccated coconut = 4¹/₂ tablespoons
1 oz cornflour = 2¹/₂ tablespoons
1 oz custard powder = 2¹/₂ tablespoons
1 oz curry powder and spices = 5 tablespoons
1 oz flour = 2 level tablespoons
1 oz rice, uncooked = 1¹/₂ tablespoons
1 oz sugar, caster and granulated = 2 tablespoons
1 oz icing sugar = 2¹/₂ tablespoons
1 oz yeast, granulated = 1 level tablespoon

American Measures

16 fl oz	=1 American pint
8 fl oz	=1 American standard cup
0.50 fl oz	=1 American tablespoon
(slightly smaller than British Standards Institute tablespoon)	
0.16 fl oz	=1 American teaspoon

Australian Cup Measures
(Using the 8-liquid-ounce cup measure)

1 cup flour	4 oz
1 cup sugar (crystal or caster)	8 oz
1 cup icing sugar (free from lumps)	5 oz
1 cup shortening (butter, margarine)	8 oz
1 cup brown sugar (lightly packed)	4 oz
1 cup soft breadcrumbs	2 oz
1 cup dry breadcrumbs	3 oz
1 cup rice (uncooked)	6 oz
1 cup rice (cooked)	5 oz
1 cup mixed fruit	4 oz
1 cup grated cheese	4 oz
1 cup nuts (chopped)	4 oz
1 cup coconut	2¹/₂ oz

Australian Spoon Measures

	level tablespoon
1 oz flour	2
1 oz sugar	1¹/₂
1 oz icing sugar	2
1 oz shortening	1
1 oz honey	1
1 oz gelatine	2
1 oz cocoa	3
1 oz cornflour	2¹/₂
1 oz custard powder	2¹/₂

Australian Liquid Measures
(Using 8-liquid-ounce cup)

1 cup liquid	8 oz
2¹/₂ cups liquid	20 oz (1 pint)
2 tablespoons liquid	1 oz
1 gill liquid	5 oz (¹/₄ pint)